TO TURN FROM IDOLS

TO TURN FROM IDOLS

by

KENNETH HAMILTON

William B. Eerdmans Publishing Company
Grand Rapids, Michigan

Library of Congress Cataloging in Publication Data

Hamilton, Kenneth.
    To turn from idols.

    Includes bibliographical references.
    1. Idols and images — Worship. 2. Christianity —
20th century. I. Title.
BL485.H35   230   73-76533
ISBN 0-8028-1528-6

First printing, August 1973
Second printing, April 1974

Chapter Four originally appeared in slightly altered form in
CHRISTIANITY TODAY, March 31, 1972. Copyright 1972 by
CHRISTIANITY TODAY; reprinted by permission.

Scripture quotations are, unless otherwise indicated, from THE
NEW ENGLISH BIBLE. Copyright © The Delegates of the Oxford
University Press and The Syndics of the Cambridge University
Press 1961, 1970. Reprinted by permission.

The chorus of LORD OF THE DANCE, by Sydney Carter,
Copyright © 1963 by Galliard Ltd. All rights reserved. Used by
permission of Galaxy Music Corp., N.Y., sole U.S. agent.

Contents

". . . how you turned from idols,
to be servants of the living and true God. . . ."

I Thess. 1:9

PREFACE

In recent years theologians have become increasingly aware of the importance of the study of language in relation to their own studies. During these years, they have also given attention to the light that world literature can shed on theological themes. An interest in both lines of approach to the theological task has brought me to attempt the present work. One cannot go far into either language or literature without being confronted by the need to say something definite about the imagination. That is what I have tried to do in this book.

Imagination, the dictionary informs us, is the power to call up images in the mind. Since "image" in the Bible refers most frequently to an idol or false image of God, I have found it natural to focus my study on the phenomenon of idolatry. Yet there are good images as well as bad ones. And there are images that in themselves are neither good nor bad but become one or the other according to how they are used. The implication of the title of this book is that one of the ways of speaking about faith is to talk of turning away from false images to true ones. Paul himself used this way of speaking when he said that God's will for those who love him is that they are to be "conformed to the image of his Son" (Rom. 8:29 KJV).

Those who wish to go straight to the central argument of the book may find it convenient to begin with Part Two, where I analyze some of the idols or false images current today, and afterwards go back to Part One, in which I trace the biblical grounds for seeing idolatry as arising out of the false images conceived in the imagination. Part Three goes on to suggest some means for combating contemporary idolatries by learning to use "good" images within the life of the Christian church.

This book has grown out of several separate studies carried on before I became aware that I was being led towards the central theme of the imagination and its images. Part Two began as a series of three talks given to the Ministers' Convocation of the National Association of Congregational Christian Churches of the United States at Milwaukee in April 1972. Part Three is based on the Berger Lectures at Dubuque Theological Seminary in February 1972. Not much of the text of the original lectures remains, though perhaps the general drift of the arguments is still recognizable. I am grateful for the kindness with which my presentations were received in both Milwaukee and Dubuque, and I benefited greatly from the discussions that followed in each case. Chapter Four originally appeared in *Christianity Today* under the title of "The Irrelevance of Relevance." It, too, is given here in a somewhat altered form.

Scriptural quotations are from the New English Bible unless otherwise indicated.

— Kenneth Hamilton

The University of Winnipeg

Part One

THE IMAGES OF IDOLATRY

1

IDOLS AND THE LIVING GOD

Are Idols Obsolete?

My theme is modern idolatry. But who worships idols any more? Of all the commandments of the Decalogue the one prohibiting graven images is the one that seems least meaningful to us today. We can understand warnings against stealing, adultery, killing, giving false evidence, and coveting. We can understand the admonition to honor our parents. These are moral issues. We can also understand the permanent validity of religious duties: to serve one God, to avoid blasphemy, and to keep prescribed holy days. But what need is there today for a commandment prohibiting idolatry? We are reasonably certain that we shall never feel any strong urge to set up an idol and bow down before it.

Perhaps the impulse to engage in idolatry has simply faded from the present-day consciousness. If so, the word "idol" has become applicable wholly to other times and other cultures. It enters our own lives simply as a metaphor rather remotely connected with its original literal sense, as when we speak of idolizing a film star or a hockey player. Taken in this figurative sense, an idol is anything at all that we value more highly than we ought to, anything that we worship — that is, ascribe worth to (*worth*-ship) — inordinately.

11

Times and customs change. Yet it is most unlikely that
idolatry, a practice so consistently and continuously condemned in the Bible as a supreme threat to true faith,
has vanished without a trace because of cultural changes.
Idols may be literally obsolete, to the extent that graven
images are no longer a familiar part of the furniture of
our Western world. But they may continue in another
form. And I believe that they do persist among us in a
form that has a genuine continuity with those old images,
not merely in a watered-down metaphorical sense.

The contention underlying the argument of this book
concerning modern idolatries is that the warning against
worship of idols given in the Second Commandment
remains very pertinent to our own culture. Our cultural
climate has altered the external face of idol-worship but
not its essential danger or seductiveness. The permanent source of the temptation to take the way of idolatry
lies in what may be called the idolatrous imagination. In
this chapter and the two following I shall try to set out a
rationale for this standpoint, and particularly for connect-
ing idolatry with the imagination.

The Dynamics of the Non-Existent

For Christians the witness of Scripture must be primary.
This chapter will concentrate primarily on the Old Testament, where the shape of the biblical protest against
idolatry is seen most clearly. But the New Testament has
one extremely illuminating passage on the subject of idolatry. This is in I Corinthians 8, where Paul discusses the
problem of Christians eating food offered to idols.

Paul begins with the opinions put forward by some of
the Corinthian Christians who hold that the issue needs no
debate. Because all Christians know the heathen gods to
be nonexistent, these men argue, they can eat meat dedicated to a god even within the pagan shrine itself. By so
doing they show their indifference to and contempt for
idolatrous superstition. But Paul thinks that this view leaves

something out. He begins by giving a warning that knowledge is not everything. Knowledge "breeds conceit," and it is love that God expects from us.

> Well then, about eating this consecrated food: of course, as you say, 'a false god has no existence in the real world. There is no god but one.' For indeed, if there be so-called gods, whether in heaven or on earth — as indeed there are many 'gods' and many 'lords' — yet for us there is one God, the Father, from whom all being comes, towards whom we move; and there is one Lord, Jesus Christ, through whom all things came to be, and we through him.
>
> But not every one knows this. There are some who have been so accustomed to idolatry that even now they eat this food with a sense of its heathen consecration, and their conscience, being weak, is polluted by the eating (vv. 4-7).

The most evident thrust in Paul's argument here is one of pastoral concern. He denies that the problem of dealing with idolatry can be solved by an act of the intellect ("knowledge") alone. Instead of suggesting that the weak Christians be educated and convinced that the consecration of food to nonexistent deities could make no difference, Paul counsels loving concern to support such persons. The Christian community must be ready to be sensitive to the needs of their consciences. An outreach of love entails entering imaginatively into the perspective of those whose intellectual background is one of paganism. Granted that idolatry traffics in gods that are actually nonexistent, these very imaginary gods are present and real to the imagination of those brought up to trust in them. Therefore the right answer theoretically may be the wrong approach personally. Using strong terms, Paul insists: "This 'knowledge' of yours is utter disaster to the weak, the brother for whom Christ died" (I Cor. 8:11).

Today, familiar with the various levels of consciousness, we may be ready to agree that Paul shows a true pastoral insight in recognizing that the strongest factors involved in belief are usually extrarational. A conscious confession of faith held as an intellectual conviction is not necessarily proof against a store of images — impressions on the

imagination — gathered over the years. Images that have
deeply affected us in the past do not wither away without
a trace, and at any time they may come flooding back
unbidden into our present. Thus, without analyzing the
psyche, Paul has a sharp perception of the harmful effects
of putting abstract reasoning before the practical psychological situation faced by recent converts from paganism.

All the same it would be rash to conclude too quickly
that Paul's pastoral advice concentrates exclusively on
psychological issues. Psychology is involved, of course.
When Paul writes about the weak conscience, he is dealing with what we today would call the subjective factors
in belief. At the same time, there is an objective reference
in his argument. His words about overestimating the value
of knowledge for the life of faith are what gives the argument its essential context. They are theological words
quite as much as psychological words, for they speak of
what the life of faith is as well as of how people are dis-
posed to view it. Paul's theological estimate of knowledge
bears on the whole question of the biblical approach to
idolatry.

The term "knowledge" *(gnosis)* is found frequently in
both I and II Corinthians, possibly because in the eyes of
the Corinthian Christians knowledge was a highly valued
mark of all true religion.[1] Paul uses the term positively.
For him, knowledge is a necessary part of the equipment
of every Christian believer. To have knowledge is to
stand firm in the faith (I Cor. 1:5). But early in the Corinthian correspondence Paul introduces an extended contrast between human and divine wisdom (I Cor. 1:17-31;
2:1-16). The introduction of this closely related theme
may well be intended to suggest that what men call knowledge may be often mere human wisdom, which God sees

---

[1]See C. K. Barrett, *The First Epistle to the Corinthians* (London: A. &
C. Black, 1968), pp. 36-37, 189-90. Barrett does not think that the high
estimate of *gnosis* among the Corinthians necessarily points to any specific
allegiance to religious gnosticism. Rather, gnostic teachings were in the
air at the time, and the ideals made popular by various gnostic sects were
currently influential even among converts to Christianity.

as folly. The argument of chapter 8 certainly gives an ironic tone to the word "knowledge." (In the New English Bible Paul's irony is brought out by twice putting the word in quotation marks: in verse one and in verse eleven.) Here, too, Paul compares knowledge unfavorably with love, as he does again in I Corinthians 13 (vv. 8f., 12).

In the context of idolatry, Paul's refusal to absolutize knowledge has important implications. For Christians, Paul makes plain, there can be the confession of one God alone, God the Father, and one Lord, Jesus Christ, who shares in God's creative work in the world and in us. That every other "god" or "lord" simply *is not* would seem to follow logically from this premise. Yet Paul seems to assign that conclusion to the realm of knowledge that leads to pride and away from love. What we have here is a reticence in drawing conclusions, which comes from Paul's recognition of something that might be termed *the dynamics of the nonexistent*. A pagan deity is literally nothing; and yet this nothing can have power over the weak conscience, and therefore has to be reckoned with. So-called knowledge fails to reckon with this power. From its altitude of intellectual security it fails to see all there is to see. Thus it withholds support from the brother whose need is real because of its confidence that there can be no threat to anyone — nothing threatens since idols are nothing.

Another way of stating the position underlying Paul's argument is to recognize that for him the confession of belief in the one true God is not to be equated with an abstract monotheism. God is the Creator who has revealed himself as the God of Israel and the Father of our Lord Jesus Christ. Confession of belief in this God is made in the obedience of outgoing love. Where such love is lacking, God has not been truly confessed. The Corinthian Christians, who prided themselves in the completeness of their knowledge, proved themselves to be lacking in loving concern for their weaker brethren. Theoretical monotheists they might be, but in practice they did not know God as he wishes himself to be known. This points to the

poverty of their "knowledge." The reality of the one true
God — and therefore the truth about idolatry — cannot
be grasped by the intellect alone.

Paul was a Hebrew of the Hebrews (Phil. 3:5). The
source for his view that the proper understanding of idolatry is not primarily an intellectual matter is thus likely to
be found in the teaching of the Old Testament.

There Is No Other

The Israelites lived in a world in which a plurality of
gods was taken for granted. They knew Yahweh — "The
LORD" — as the God who had promised to protect and
guide their nation.[2] They recognized their special obligation to worship him, just as they recognized that each of
their neighbor nations had its special deity. Their great
fear was to be left without a god to look after them, a
god whom they could be sure of at all times, a god whom

[2]See the translators' introduction to the Old Testament of the New English Bible on the divine name *YHWH*, which is normally indicated in
the NEB by "LORD" or "GOD" in capital letters. It is essential to
recognize that "The LORD" is in the Bible God's personal name and not
a general title.

For a long time the word "God" has been considered a common noun
and not a proper noun. The intellectual climate of our culture has taken
over the concept which Paul refers to when he speaks of "many 'gods'
and many 'lords,' " making this the norm for interpreting the word "God."
This common usage has immensely impoverished our vocabulary in relation to the Bible. It has taken away to a large extent also the unique,
personal reality of the name "The LORD." When we wish to make plain
that we are referring to The LORD and not just to any "god," we are
driven to make use of such phrases as "the God of the Bible" or "the
Christian God." Such phrases still suggest that the primary meaning of
the word "God" is a general one, and that we are referring to one member of a class. Thus we are driven by language to indulge in a verbal idolatry, confessing the (possible) existence of many gods and many lords.
There are occasions when this linguistic polytheism or agnosticism is right
and proper, but the occasion of interpreting the Bible is not one of them.

In the circumstances, it is understandable why the Jerusalem Bible,
among modern translations, has used the name "Yahweh" in place of the
more traditional "The Lord." The New English Bible's choice of "The
LORD" is a compromise that at least draws attention to the fact that this
title is more than a title — it indicates one who is unique and not simply
a member of a class made up of many "lords."

they could call their own. So whenever things started to go wrong with them, they were tempted to imagine that Yahweh had ceased to be their very own, trustworthy deity; and their fearfulness caused them to turn elsewhere for assurance. That is why Aaron made a golden calf for them at Sinai. Moses' long delay in the mountain had made them suspect that they had been left unprotected (Exod. 32:1-6). Similarly, Ezekiel records that when idols were set up within the Temple after the fall of Jerusalem this was because those who were left there had begun to believe themselves cut off from Yahweh and no more regarded by him. "They think that the LORD does not see them, or that he has forsaken the country" (Ezek. 8:12).

The primary work of the prophets of Israel was to insist on the utter dependability of Israel's God, on his power and willingness to care for his people. Another god might have become tired of such fickleness and faithlessness as Israel had shown time and again. But Yahweh was not like other gods. He had chosen Israel without regard for any qualities she possessed, and he never would go back on his covenant love for her. At the time of the Exodus from Egypt he had proved his superiority to all other gods. In every other crisis for the nation he would prove equally resourceful, equally triumphant.

Paul's distinction between love and knowledge can be seen to have its origins in Old Testament revelation. To love Yahweh, the one Lord, with heart and soul and strength (Deut. 6:4, 5) was the obedience required of Israel. Israel had to learn to say, "For us there is one God." For a long time Israel's "knowledge" did not include the ability to assert the absolute nonexistence of other gods. It was enough to obey the command to have no other gods "to set against" Yahweh (Exod. 20:3; Deut. 5:7) and to know the defender of Israel to be Yahweh, the God of gods (Josh. 22:22). The claim of obedience was paramount, as Elijah showed in his challenge to the priests of Baal on Mount Carmel. There Elijah told the people that they had to make a plain choice between Baal and Yahweh; while they tried to resist that choice by remaining silent (I Kings 18:21).

The increase in Israel's "knowledge" to the point where the actuality of other gods could be denied came through a long process of education of Israel's imagination rather than through a direct appeal to the intellect. The Book of Isaiah is often cited as being the decisive proclamation of monotheism. Certainly, this book carries an unmistakable message of Yahweh's sole rule over all things in heaven and earth. The message is heard especially in the great forty-fifth chapter with its refrain, "I am the LORD, there is no other" (vv. 5, 6, 14, 18, 21, 22, 24). In Isaiah's prophetic teaching the idolater is not only a religious apostate, a turner aside to "strange" gods. He is also a ridiculous figure. Idols, being human artifacts, are manifestly not divine; and to put one's trust in them is to outrage common sense.

To speak of Isaiah as teaching "monotheism" may be formally correct. Yahweh's sole Lordship seems to have been taken into the intellectual sphere and made into a principle of knowledge as well as one of practical fidelity. But the term "monotheism" really fits our modern mental perspective better than it does that of the world to which Isaiah addressed himself. The stress throughout the biblical book is always on Yahweh's marvelous power and his perennial concern for his people. The exaltation of Israel's God as the personal, creative source of all that has ever existed or can exist in no way annuls the truth that he remains the self-revealing God, the holy one of Israel. There is no knowledge of him to be found except through the obedient reception of his word as and when he wills to speak to his people (Isa. 55:8-12).

There is no thought here that men can conclude for themselves that the universe requires a single Prime Mover or First Cause. Rather, the command to acknowledge no other god over against Yahweh has been taken to its furthest extent, leaving no room for any being in heaven or on earth except Yahweh the Creator and those beings he has called into existence. Perhaps there is a genuine intellectual implication in Isaiah's description of the LORD, the first and the last, "who has summoned the generations from the beginning" (Isa. 41:4). The description itself, however, is imaginative, not argumentative, in its appeal. By piling a wealth of vivid images one on another, Isaiah seeks to awaken an awed reverence before this God whose majesty is so overwhelming that other gods are simply crowded out of the picture. "There is no other" is not the conclusion of a syllogism. The words form part of God's self-revelation, a revelation declaring that the holy one of Israel claims for himself everything that the word "god" can possibly mean. There is no remainder. Nothing that pertains to divinity is to be found anywhere else.

A noteworthy feature of Isaiah's presentation is his continued care to rebut the belief that had from earliest times been the cause of Israel's turning away to worship foreign gods, the belief that Yahweh has ceased to care for his people. Writing of the Creator's unlimited and unwearied activity, Isaiah asks:

> Why do you complain, O Jacob,
> And you, Israel, why do you say,
> 'My plight is hidden from the LORD
> and my cause has passed out of God's notice'?
>
> (40:27)

From the same perspective, the "nothingness" of idols is deduced from the observation that they are unable to help their worshipers:

> Do what you can, good or ill,
> anything that may grip us with fear and awe.
> You cannot! You are sprung from nothing,
> your works are rotten;
> . . . .
> Nothing that they do has any worth,
> their effigies are wind, mere nothings.
>
> (41:23-24, 29)

The case for "monotheism," indeed, is argued no differently by Isaiah than it was by Elijah on Mount Carmel. That is to say, it is not supported by an appeal to the illumination of the mind by "knowledge." Either Israel puts her entire trust in Israel's God or she does not. If she does, there is room for no other god. If she does not, she has to learn her folly in trusting those who are no gods. Left defenseless, she has to find her way back in repentance to the holy one who alone guides her and controls her destiny according to his almighty will. The choice is the same as that which the Book of Deuteronomy records in the words of Moses to the people before they entered the Promised Land:

> I offer you the choice of life or death, blessing or curse. Choose life and then you and your descendants will live; love the LORD your God, obey him and hold fast to him; that is life for you and length of days in the land which the LORD swore to give your fathers, Abraham, Isaac, and Jacob (30:19-20).

The Changeless God and Changing Idols

In the Bible, then, the "nothingness" of idols is never asserted as a general truth to be known by itself. The non-existence of the gods of the Gentiles is always made plain in the context of obedient love to the God who reveals himself as sufficient in and by his power to look after his own. Another way of saying this is that the Second Commandment is a corollary of the First. The prohibition against making graven images follows from the injunction not to have any god to set against the God of Israel.[3]

You shall have no other god to set against me (Exod.

[3]In the Roman and Lutheran traditions the prohibition of graven images is considered to be part of the First Commandment. The issue, however, is not how the Ten Commandments are most conveniently divided into ten individual commandments. What is important is for the commandments to be seen as a unity, not as a collection of separate religious and moral precepts. The presupposition that Yahweh alone is to be worshiped and that his commands alone have binding force on Israel is the foundation on which the Ten Commandments are built. The occasional attempt to show that the commandments are a list of "natural" or "timeless" principles applicable to good order in any community is fundamentally mistaken. The Bible never accommodates itself to this kind of timelessness. It is too firmly rooted in the actualities of history.

20:3; Deut. 5:7). Because this commandment was directed
to call forth the obedience of Israel by reminding them
of Yahweh's supreme power and constant care, it remained unaffected by changes in Israel's culture and the
intellectual climate of the times. It did not matter greatly
whether the people believed that the gods of the nations
had some kind of independent existence or whether they
were pure fictions, empty "wind." Paul's affirmation,
"For us there is one God," sufficed in every generation
to answer the essential question about where a man's
loyalty must be placed. The intellectual interpretation of
the being of other gods was always secondary. What was
of first importance was to recognize their powerlessness
over against the one who ruled in heaven and on earth,
and to realize the enormity of the faithlessness involved
in turning to them from the living God who had given so
many evidences of his care. The folly and ignorance of
the idolater was grounded in his blindness to these realities.

Even when Israel developed a concept of wisdom, it
was understood that all wisdom flowed from God and was
learned in obedience to him. Human wisdom, apart from
the knowledge of Yahweh, was foolishness; for in fear of
him began both wisdom and knowledge (Ps. 111:10;
Prov. 1:7; 9:10). Paul appeals explicitly to this Old Testament understanding of wisdom when he speaks of the
wisdom of men as foolishness in the eyes of God (I Cor.
1:17-31). The same thought is implicitly present when he
refers in chapter 8 ironically to the "knowledge" on
which the Corinthians so prided themselves — a knowledge wholly different in kind from that praised in the
Old Testament. It is instructive that, when Paul mentions
the contrast between human and divine wisdom, he links
with it the contrast between human and divine strength
(I Cor. 1:25, 27). For the all-sufficiency of Yahweh's
power as the final explanation of his government of the
world open to Israel's understanding is as prominent in
the Wisdom literature as it is in the rest of the Old Testament. The Book of Job ends with the justification of
Job because Job repents having spoken "of great things

which I have not understood" (Job 42:3). His "ignorant words" are overwhelmed by the omnipotence of his maker.

The all-sufficiency of the one God is the constant factor in the biblical polemic against idolatry, since this is what idolaters who turn to "other gods" fail to understand. Throughout the whole biblical period idol-worship was the most pervasive feature of Gentile religion, so it is small wonder that in both the Old and the New Testaments the graven image is identified with faithlessness to the Creator.[4]

Images made by men, however, are not entirely the sole stimulus to idolatry known in the Bible. In the Old Testament there are some references also to the worship of natural phenomena. Jeremiah, for example, warns his countrymen against being awed, as the nations are, by "signs in the heavens" — evidently the stars (Jer. 10:2). Ezekiel presents a series of scenes describing the profanation of the Temple by idolatry. The series culminates in a view of twenty-five men, with their backs to the sanctuary and their faces to the east, worshiping the rising sun (Ezek. 8:16). Ezekiel evidently regards this as the ultimate profanation. In the Apocrypha, though, there is a new development. The Wisdom of Solomon speaks of two grades of idolaters. Those who worship images are supremely culpable, for they attribute power to "dead things." Those who worship the elements, while guilty of not rising from the Creator's handiwork to the Creator himself, are less degraded. These have been impressed at least by the power and beauty of the created order (Wisd. 13 & 14).

The Book of Wisdom shows strong continuity with the Old Testament in its descriptions of the futility of image-worship. But the relative mildness of its comments on the worship of the elements and the stars seems to indicate the influence of Greek culture; or perhaps it may represent an attempt to speak to that culture. Astrology was rampant among the Greeks. The gods of Olympus were

[4]Because they refused to pay homage to any image and had none of their own, the early Christians were often accused of being atheists.

identified with the planets, and many of the characters of Greek mythology with the other stars. In itself this would not have made star-veneration less obnoxious to the Hebrews, who were familiar with astral deities from Babylonia — the ultimate source, incidentally, of Greek astrology. From the time of Plato, however, educated Greeks had regarded the gods as aspects of a single supreme deity. Indeed, monotheism as an intellectual system may be said to have been invented by the Greek mind. Israel worshiped one God. The Greek philosophers and their disciples, on the other hand, did not consider worship to be very important. They regarded it mostly as a social duty. Yet, while quite willing to honor the gods according to established custom, they rejected polytheism as a viable interpretation of the universe. To a Hellenized Jew, philosophical monotheism — or other beliefs that tended in that direction — were clearly superior to crude idol-worship.

Now, this is a very different viewpoint from that of the Old Testament. There Moses, after forbidding image-making, went on at once to say:

> Nor must you raise your eyes to the heavens and look up to the sun, the moon, and the stars, all the hosts of heaven, and be led to bow down to them and worship them; the LORD your God assigned these for the worship of the various peoples under heaven (Deut. 4:19).

The thought that the worship of the host of heaven might be a halfway house between thoroughgoing idolatry and the pure worship of the living God was one hardly conceivable before the Hebrews were exposed to Greek culture, and were forced to come to terms with it to a greater or a lesser degree.

It was within this new cultural context, nevertheless, that Christianity was born. When the people of Israel — and later the young Christian church — became geographically and culturally intermingled with the nations even though conscious of being religiously distinct from them, the "signs in the heavens" that awed the nations

took on a new importance. The result was to affect very
drastically how the Judeo-Christian faith explained itself;
since it now spoke in the presence of a Gentile audience
and, so far as the Christian church was concerned, was a
body made up largely of converts from paganism who
retained many pagan presuppositions. Changing religious
beliefs in the Greco-Roman world, too, made the confrontation between different faiths take on a new com-
plexity. The simple identification of idolatry with graven
images was no longer a cultural reality.

2

THE IDOLATROUS IMAGINATION

The Tyranny of the Abstract Powers

Although in New Testament times the gods of paganism still maintained their popular appeal and images were omnipresent, the power of polytheistic religion over men's imaginations was waning. The Acts of the Apostles, for instance, tells the story of the riot in Ephesus led by Demetrius the silversmith in protest against Christian condemnation of idols (Acts 19:23-41). It is clear that religious zeal was the least element in the opposition to Paul's preaching, and clear also that the town official was personally skeptical that any sacrilege was involved. A little earlier there is recorded the interesting incident of Ephesian converts to Christianity publicly burning their privately owned books of magic (Acts 19:18-20). These books of "magical spells" were largely connected with astrology; and they probably represented the real religious interest of many of the citizens of Ephesus.

In his informative study of Pauline theology G. B. Caird gives an account of the consequences of the growing importance of astrology in the Greco-Roman world. He writes:

> With the advent of astrology the anthropomorphic gods had begun to give place to "the army of unalterable law." The iron

rule of an impersonal fate robbed life both of meaning and hope, and no small part of the appeal of Paul's preaching must have been that it offered release from servitude to the elemental spirits. Yet at the same time astrology with its reign of law gave to the polytheistic world a valuable preparation for the coming of a monotheistic religion.[1]

Exposed to the Hellenistic cultural environment, Judaism also gave great prominence to the presence of elemental spirits and superhuman powers. Yet there was an important contrast between Greek and Jewish attitudes. Pagan thought conceived these powers as abstract and inexorable in their impact on human destiny. In Hebrew thought, on the other hand, they were personalized and subject to the Creator, even though they rebelliously worked against his good ordering of the world. Speaking of Paul's doctrine of the "principalities and powers," Caird notes how "in Jewish belief the pagan gods were in reality angelic beings to whom God had delegated some measure of his own authority, but whose character had become corrupted by an idolatrous worship, which exalted them to a divine and absolute status."[2]

The outcome of this contrast was that the Greek and the Hebrew views of the universe, while they might seem to approach each other on the level of "knowledge," remained completely opposed on the level of living faith. The Greco-Roman world was a near-despairing one, dominated as it was by the twin powers of Necessity and Chance. And here — as Caird indicates — the preaching of the early Christians brought a message of hope that spoke to the pagan condition. For the Christian church was rooted in the Old Testament Scriptures and their call to trust in the supreme power of the living God. No angel, no power, no so-called god, no created thing could

[1] *Principalities and Powers* (Oxford: Clarendon Press, 1956), p. 51.

[2] *Ibid.*, pp. 48-49. Similarly, Jean Héring in his examination of Paul's words about "many gods and many lords" in I Corinthians 8:5 concludes: "In short, the Apostle denies the existence of pagan gods, but admits that there are angelic powers, though they must not be worshipped whatever the name that is given to them" (*The First Epistle of Saint Paul to the Corinthians,* London: Epworth Press, 1962, p. 69).

ever come between us and the one God whose love had
been made visible in Jesus Christ (Rom. 8:38-39 — see
the Jerusalem Bible translation). Within the Christian
community the First Commandment was seen to be as
pertinent as ever in the context of contemporary culture.
And Christians remembered how their Lord during his
temptations in the wilderness had quoted the exposition
of it (Deut. 6:13) against Satan's lying promises. Jesus
had answered: "Scripture says, 'You shall do homage to
the LORD your God and worship him alone' " (Luke 4:8).

In face of a contrast so complete it may be somewhat
misleading to look at the pagan shift from anthropomorphic gods to impersonal powers as chiefly a preparation
for monotheistic religion. Their dissatisfaction with polytheistic crudities brought some educated pagans to consider
seriously the claims of both Judaism and Christianity.
Several of the early church fathers were converted philosophers who wished to bridge the gap between pagan speculative knowledge and the saving knowledge they had found
in Christ. Yet the gap was a real one, and crossing it en-
tailed a radical conversion. On Mars Hill there was little
response from the philosophically minded among the
listeners to Paul's apologetic efforts to speak of the one
God on the basis of the pagan search for the unknown
god. The problem was that these "cultured despisers"
of popular polytheistic religion found Paul's language
about the living God and his actions in the world to be
unbelievably anthropomorphic. A god who summoned a
"world come of age" to leave behind the times of ignorance when images were worshiped was one thing. But a
god who had appointed a time when he would judge mankind through the agency of a man whom he had raised
from the dead (Acts 17:30-31) was quite another thing.
Seemingly, the advance in "knowledge" that Paul had
offered with one hand he had taken away with his other;
and his "new" teaching had proved to be nothing more
than a mishmash of old superstitions. So the Athenian
intelligentsia turned away scoffing.

Perhaps Paul's experience at Athens persuaded him to

preach Christ crucified without regard to the Greek search
for intellectual truth. He would have to declare "the
attested truth of God without display of fine words or
wisdom," even though the contemporary world considered
the message to be folly (I Cor. 1:22; 2:1). The final justification for faith could not be "human wisdom" but
"the power of God" (I Cor. 2:5). Thus Paul followed
the path taken by the writers of the Old Testament —
proclaiming the one God's message to his people by
witnessing to his acts on their behalf, instead of by trying
to explain on general principles why it was reasonable to
believe in him.

Whatever the causes for Paul's approach to his missionary task, he spoke to the needs of the day. An abstract monotheism was no nearer to Christian faith than
a naive polytheism had been, for it delivered men from
bondage to nonexistent gods only to turn them over to the
tyranny of abstract powers and invisible forces. Ordinary
men might seek to bend the cosmic powers to their own
advantage through magic, while philosophers believed
them to be the primal laws built into the structure of the
universe itself. Either way, these powers were fearsome
in reducing individual human lives to insignificance and
impotence. By insisting that "the powers that rule the'
world" (I Cor. 2:8) were simply agents of the Creator
— rebellious agents, yet always accountable to God's
supreme will — Paul robbed them of their paralyzing
grip on men's imaginations. They were relative, not
absolute rulers. Consequently, the universe became a
place where personal purpose reigned instead of an impersonal, implacable order that turned men into pawns
in a cosmic game. To the Christians at Rome Paul wrote:
"The Spirit you have received is not a spirit of slavery
leading you back into a life of fear, but a Spirit that
makes us sons, enabling us to cry 'Abba! Father' " (Rom.
8:15). It had been the personal action of the Father
through the Spirit that had raised Christ Jesus from the
dead; and now this same Spirit was being given to bring

new life to those who had been justified by faith in
Christ (Rom. 8:10-11).

The antidote to fear of the abstract powers was the
concrete revelation in Christ of the living God, the Creator still personally active in his world. "For the same
God who said, 'Out of darkness let light shine', has
caused his light to shine within us, to give the light of
revelation — the revelation of the glory of God in the
face of Jesus Christ" (II Cor. 4:6).

"The Imagination of Men's Hearts"

The Bible refers often to human ways of thinking that
are ignorant of and in opposition to God's truth. Several
forms of expression are used for this, in both Hebrew
and Greek, but the King James Version usually renders
these references by variations on the phrase "the imagination of men's hearts" (Gen. 6:21; Deut. 29:19; I Chron.
28:9; Prov. 6:18; Jer. 23:17; Luke 1:51). Modern translations attempt to render this more precisely as "inclina-
tions" or "mind" or "the invention of men's thoughts"
or "promptings of their own stubborn hearts." But the
translators of 1611 performed a valuable service to all
Bible readers in using a constant form of phrase.

In the seventeenth century the word "imagination"
was connected with unreality. It suggested the imaginary
rather than the imaginative. For example, the Duke of
Athens in Shakespeare's *A Midsummer-Night's Dream*
observes:

> Lovers and madmen have such seething brains,
> Such shaping fantasies, that apprehend
> More than cool reason ever comprehends.
> The lunatic, the lover, and the poet,
> Are of imagination all compact;
>
> . . . .
> Such tricks hath strong imagination,
> That, if it would but apprehend some joy,
> It comprehends some bringer of that joy;
> Or in the night, imagining some fear,
> How easy is a bush suppos'd a bear!
>
> (Act V, Scene i, 4-8, 18-22)

Thus the seventeenth-century translators of the Bible could be sure that their phrase "the imagination of men's hearts" would be understood to mean men's foolish fancies. The consistent judgment of Scripture is that man makes his own road maps to hell. Unwilling to be led by revealed truth, he shapes reality according to some pattern spun out of his own head; and the resulting picture bears no relation to things as they really are. The Creator sees these spurious "creations" of the human mind and pronounces them to be falsely and arrogantly conceived.

Even in the seventeenth century, all the same, it was recognized that imagination could play a constructive as well as a deceptive role in human affairs. The most frequently quoted part of the speech cited above describes the poetic imagination:

> The poet's eye, in a fine frenzy rolling,
> Doth glance from heaven to earth, from earth to heaven;
> And, as imagination bodies forth
> The forms of things unknown, the poet's pen
> Turns them to shapes, and gives to airy nothing
> A local habitation and a name.
>
> *(Loc. cit.,* 12-17)

Shakespeare is somewhat tongue-in-cheek when comparing the poet's ability to invent verbal images with the "frenzy" of the lunatic and the lover, for he knows that the poet's function is to interpret human experience as accurately and intimately as possible. Far from being the dupe of imagination's "tricks," the poet uses his imaginative talents to make a true report on the world. The imagination,\ in short, can be used either to enlighten or to delude. Everything depends upon how it is used.

Not only poetic imagination "gives to airy nothing /A local habitation and a name." All imagination does that. In the previous chapter we saw that an idol may be "nothing" and yet be real to the imaginations of individuals.[3] This is an instance of "shaping fantasies, that apprehend / More than cool reason ever comprehends."

[3]See above, pp. 12-16.

Shakespeare's distinction between *app*rehend and *com*-prehend is useful: "apprehension" signifies expectation, and "comprehension" signifies believing to be actually present and real. The Corinthian Christians who prided themselves on their "knowledge" were certain that their weaker brethren were misled by their apprehension and so did not comprehend the nothingness of idols. They themselves, guided by "cool reason," comprehended the truth perfectly.

There is always a possibility, just the same, that cool reason is too cool and too unimaginative. If overactive imagination can result in wrong comprehension, reason overconfident of itself can end up equally wide of the mark through inadequate apprehension. Poverty of the imagination may prove as fatal as imagination run wild. Common sense rightly pillories foolish fears capable of turning a harmless bush into a bear, but an inexperienced city dweller out in the wilds has to be warned that a bear sometimes looks like a bush. And not all questions of truth and error lend themselves to be so easily resolved as this one. Again, Shakespeare puts the issue memorably:

> There are more things in heaven and earth, Horatio,
> Than are dreamt of in your philosophy.
> (Hamlet, Act I, Scene v, 166-67)

A credulity that believes everything is no less foolish than a skeptical rationalism shut up within its own presuppositions that mistakes the walls raised by its dogmas for the horizons of reality. It is easy to say, "Nothing here!" and to ignore the dynamics of the nonexistent.[4]

In this connection we should be aware that inadequate

---

[4]There is an interesting parallel between Paul's treatment of the question of idols in I Corinthians and Shakespeare's treatment of the ghost of Hamlet's father. Hamlet's belief that he has been talking to the ghost prompts him to address the familiar words to Horatio about "more things in heaven and earth." The existence of ghosts was as disputed a topic in Elizabethan England as was the existence of pagan gods in first-century Corinth. Some critics believe that Horatio represents the "enlightened" Protestant opinion of the day, denying all reality to ghosts (see J. Dover Wilson, *What Happened in Hamlet*, Cambridge: Cambridge U. P., 1951,

imagination is imagination still. Every doctrinaire philosophy claims to know with certainty; yet the "knowledge"
it advances is really an imaginative picture of reality that
leaves out too much to be able to convince any but the
indoctrinated. Such philosophies are often called ideologies.
It should be realized, however, that behind the *idea* informing every ideology there lies an imaginative *picture*
of the universe. To take two obvious examples: Marxism
pictures the world as progressing under the guidance of
the material life-process; racism pictures the world as
producing various distinct strains of "blood," the higher
of which are contaminated when intermixed with lower
strains.

The philosophies we speak of as ideological rest on
obviously restricted imaginative apprehensions that render
them widely questionable — and widely supported, too,
since any easily grasped picture of the universe has a
popular appeal. But every philosophical or religious
doctrine presupposes some particular and selective apprehension. What it "knows" depends on what it pictures
imaginatively, that is, on its "images."

The world of the New Testament, which was experiencing a shift from fear of many gods to fear of abstract
powers, was going through a transition stage in imaginative apprehension. It was forming a new picture of the

pp. 52-78). Shakespeare does not compel us to adopt any dogmatic stand
on the subject. Of course, the ghost does appear as a *dramatis persona* on
the stage; yet he *may* be simply a product of Hamlet's distraught imagination carried away by the reports of an apparition resembling his father
having been seen on the castle walls. Hamlet has no sure "knowledge"
that the words he has heard from the ghost are true. Yet he cannot suppose
the ghost to be "nothing" or its words without significance. In the end he
does what he feels it to be his duty to do as a son who owes loyalty to his
father above his own life. Like Paul, he knows that obedient love must
take precedent to "knowledge."

Obviously, this parallel cannot be pressed too far. Belief in ghosts is not
the same thing as belief in the power of pagan deities. Faith in God is not
the same thing as filial loyalty. Shakespeare's insight into the human condition is not the same thing as biblical truth. At the same time, Shakespeare's dramatic presentation of how personal decisions must go beyond
"knowledge" and rest on "love" can open our imaginations to the issues
raised by Paul.

universe. How complete was this change? How did it impinge on contemporary Christian faith? These are important questions for us to ask, for many features of this change in apprehension are still with us. And the forms taken by the imagination of men's hearts affect twentieth-century Christianity just as they affected Judaism and the Christian church in the first century.

The Demythologizing Imagination

When the anthropomorphic gods of Greco-Roman culture began to lose their hold over men's imaginations in favor of impersonal powers, an intellectual phenomenon appeared on the scene that we know today as demythologizing. Zeus, originally the father of the gods, came to symbolize the rule of law throughout nature. Similarly, the Fates and the goddesses of Fortune, Law, Justice, Retribution, and the rest passed into general concepts about the human condition.

Largely as a result of Rudolf Bultmann's theories about the New Testament, a great deal has been written in recent years on the subject of demythologizing. What demythologizing is may be readily understood in Bultmann's terms: the removal of an understanding of the universe that is controlled by supernatural beings, and of the cosmology (a three-storied structure of heaven, earth, and hell) associated with this understanding.[5] The central question about demythologizing, though, has seldom been asked: *What does demythologizing claim to achieve?* And the answer here would seem to be that it claims to put naive and primitive statements into believable terms for sophisticated minds. In other words, it wants to substitute "cool reason" for "shaping fantasies," true comprehension for wild apprehension.

The next question is whether such a claim to "interpret" picture-language in conceptual terms is not itself rather

[5]See "New Testament and Mythology" in *Kerygma and Myth*, ed. Hans-Werner Bartsch (New York: Harper, 1961), p. 1.

naive. In every claim to comprehend — to have knowledge — it is necessary to ask what the comprehender
apprehends. What is the imaginative picture of the universe that lies behind his conceptual terms? We must ask,
then, about the driving force that activates the demythologizing imagination.

The overwhelming conviction of the demythologizing
imagination is that, by substituting abstract images for
concrete ones, it has arrived at final, unshakable knowledge. The demythologizer thinks of himself as a judge,
sitting in the seat of final wisdom, dividing truth from
error on behalf of less enlightened persons, who cannot
distinguish between appearance and reality. He is certain
that there is no questionable presupposition in his own
image of the world, that both his apprehension and his
comprehension of reality are complete. Thus the demythologizer needs to confirm his own present state of wisdom by demonstrating continuously how it contrasts with
previous ignorance. So long as attention is concentrated
on his work of correcting the presuppositions of the unenlightened past, his own presuppositions will not be called
in question.

The demythologizing imagination, in short, feeds on
beliefs that it rejects. It reacts against a polytheistic reading of the universe and drives towards abstract monotheism
— the recognition of a single power controlling all
things. It also reacts against a personalized view of existence and conceives of the universe as under the direction
of a god *(theos)* or supreme power that is wholly impersonal and not to be known through personal encounter.

The demythologizer does not break with polytheism,
as the Old Testament faith did when it confessed that no
other god was to be set against the God of Israel. The
demythologizer argues that polytheistic religions came
nearer to the truth than they knew. There are indeed
various types of power manifest in the world. Polytheists
simply failed to understand that these powers were not
separate divinities but really different aspects of one
power. Polytheists similarly understood images of the gods

to be deities locally present and potent. Actually, these were simply symbols — temporal manifestations of the nontemporal universal power that flows through all things. This power cannot itself be "imaged," because it lies beyond the senses and belongs to the realm of pure intelligibility. So, according to the demythologizer, the imagination of the polytheists was not far astray. Their apprehension was admirable, even though their comprehension required correction. They had a true, if inadequate, faith. It was knowledge that they lacked.[6]

Faith in Knowledge

The abstract monotheism of the demythologizer, therefore, does not prevent him from being imaginatively akin to that polytheism which he "interprets" in order to bring it into line with his "knowledge." The demythologizer imagines that wisdom is struggling to be born in the imagination of men's hearts, and needs only adequate "understanding" to bring it forth complete and entire. Even when he claims to "interpret" Christian faith by transposing its mythic language, his imagination follows the same line.

This can be seen from the example of Rudolf Bultmann. Bultmann contends that the language of the New Testament is mythological because it presents a view of the universe literally unbelievable to modern man. It speaks of angels and demons, of a divine man miraculously raised from the dead, and of an anthropomorphic God acting directly and arbitrarily in the world. All this flies in the face of the scientific view of universal causality. Bultmann agrees with the scientific agnostic that there is no room for an "objective" personal God in the universe as we know it. But he believes that a causality is operative in the universe other than the one recognized by science,

[6]See the defenses of image-worship by Dio Chrysostom, Maximus of Tyre, Plotinus, and Porphyry, as described by Edwyn Bevan in *Holy Images: An Inquiry into Idolatry and Image-Worship in Ancient Paganism and in Christianity* (London: Allen & Unwin, 1940), pp. 70-77.

and that is the human consciousness. He finds a clear apprehension of this free and responsible causality shining through the unreliable imagination of the New Testament writers. The comprehension of this unique causality he discovers set forth in Heidegger's philosophy of human existence. Armed with this "knowledge" provided by Heidegger, he can then proceed to affirm what it is that the New Testament "really" says through its mythic images. The words seem to refer to the acts of an objectivized God, whom we know to be nonexistent. But we should regard the words as correct *apprehension* ignorantly *comprehended*. The intention of the words, when we have stripped away their husk of myth, is to disclose "man's understanding of himself."[7]

Bultmann speaks of the need for "pre-understanding" when we approach the New Testament. No doubt this is another way of stating that we today possess full "knowledge" of what the primitive religious apprehension of the first-century Christians grasped. We know what the early Christians "really" intended to convey but could express solely through the cloudy images of myth. Bultmann, moreover, emphasizes how the essence of mythological language lies in its speaking of the divine in terms drawn from "this world." He does not mean by "this world" the New Testament concept of creaturehood in rebellion against the Creator — as in Paul's expression "the rulers of this world." Bultmann means the earth which "is the Lord's" (Ps. 24:1), the heavens which "tell out the glory of God" (Ps. 19:1). The created order, seemingly, chiefly misleads us about God. It obstructs the knowledge that a "nonobjective" God meets the world at the single point where man recognizes his own special form of being. Because today we have the pre-understanding to avoid the confusions of myth, we are happily delivered from the image of an objective and a personal God. In his essay "The Idea of God and Modern Man" Bultmann writes:

Only the idea of God which can find, which can seek and find,

7"New Testament and Mythology," *loc. cit.*, p. 10.

the unconditional in the conditional, the beyond in the here, the transcendent in the present at hand, as possibility of encounter, is possible for modern man.[8]

Bultmann, obviously, imagines that modern man has knowledge that makes it impossible for him to believe in any God who is not an abstract power, an idea that "encounters" the human consciousness as thinking in images is discarded.[9]

Demythologizers, whether they live in the first century or the twentieth, scoff at anthropomorphic gods and all "mythical" notions like the raising of the dead — when these are literally believed. But they find permanent religious value in them as myths open to interpretation through "knowledge." Then the God imaged by man stands revealed as God present in man's self-understanding, and the dying-and-rising divine man emerges as the symbol of man made aware of his own authentic being. Demythologizers *know* that naive religions are true to the extent that they reflect the genuine imagination of men's hearts, and untrue only to the extent that they rely on images drawn from the "objective" world. Yet, after all, this "knowledge" itself has no other foundation than that of the imagination of the demythologizer's heart. The demythologizing imagination is so boundless in its claims to omniscience that it can be answered only as Job answered his friends:

> No doubt you are perfect men
> and absolute wisdom is yours!
> But I have sense as well as you.
>
> (Job 12:2-3)

[8]Rudolf Bultmann *et al., Translating Theology into the Modern Age* (N.Y.: Harper & Row, 1965), p. 94 — italics in the text.

[9]In *Words and the Word* (Grand Rapids: Eerdmans, 1971), pp. 36-41, I argued that Bultmann's interpretation of Christian faith belongs to the "idealistic" tradition of philosophical thought, which believes that the divine is resident in man's consciousness to the extent that this consciousness frees itself from the phenomenal world and becomes aware of its grounding in, and its aspiration towards, "imageless transcendence." In this tradition an "idea" is never fully realized so long as it remains a detached theory or opinion. It must be the indubitable "knowledge" that comes from the encounter of man with the divine beyond all images of earth.

Irony cannot be demythologized. And irony was one of the Old Testament writers' chief weapons for attacking idolatry.

The Idolatrous Imagination

The demythologizer's uncritical faith in "knowledge" keeps him from recognizing the strength of imagination, both in himself and in others. He fails to see how pervasive and how pertinacious are imaginative images, and how frail in comparison are all intellectual systems and philosophies.

In this connection it is evident that, on the imaginative level, it often does not matter greatly whether an individual is a polytheist or assents to an abstract monotheism. The vision of the universe in which he puts his trust will be much the same in its imaginative force even though the make-up of his picture of the universe may seem very different in intellectual terms.

For example, a man may believe that there is a deity called Luck, who rewards his worshipers. Or he may just "trust his luck" without any such accompanying belief — though he will very likely follow some ritual action in order to keep luck on his side. It is socially interesting whether such a person belongs to a culture that provides him with a shrine dedicated to Luck where he can go to make his offering, or whether he instead visits a fortune teller or reads a newspaper column for advice about lucky and unlucky days. On a psychological level, too, the individual will feel differently when he is joining in a recognized cult from when, against a background of skepticism, he has to excuse his practices with the plea, "I know it sounds silly, but there may just be something to it." But whatever the specific images that come into his mind as he contemplates the world about him, the quality of his imagination will be the same. The imagination of his heart has made luck into a mighty power having control over his life.

Because the imaginative approach to the universe goes much further and deeper than any acquired "knowledge" and holds us much more strongly, we can always rationalize our beliefs with very little trouble. In general we are more ready to jettison "knowledge" than to labor to make our imaginatively conceived convictions look intellectually respectable. Today, with astrology holding such a wide influence over the imagination, one sometimes hears the objection that a superstitious belief in the influence of the stars has no possible foundation in science. The rejoinder is almost invariably along the lines: "Well, I don't think science has all the answers." Those apologists for astrology who write or lecture on the topic perhaps attempt some kind of formal argument. They explain that astrology is as much a science as astronomy, only it operates in another field. Even so, they usually spend little time on intellectual justification. It is understood well enough how difficult a thing it is to remove age-old images from men's hearts. Indoctrinate a few generations with the dogmas that experimental science has a monopoly on "knowledge" and that nothing is "real" unless attested by scientific research. A little disillusionment over the failure of the scientific community to bring to fruition the utopia promised by some of its over-enthusiastic members is all that is needed for the appeal of ancient "wisdom" to win over large numbers from their trust in modern "knowledge."

In the light of this kind of experience, solemn pronouncements about what is possible or impossible for contemporary man to believe become at once comic and pathetic. If any one generalization can be made about that almost-certainly-mythical creature "contemporary man," it is that he probably has a greater variety of beliefs than his forefathers.

The recent explosion of odd and often archaic religious beliefs, especially among the young, points to a break-up — or at the very least a severe questioning — of abstract monotheism.[10] Of course, the dominance of such mono-

---

[10]We shall be returning to this topic later. See below, pp. 166-69.

theism was never absolute. Its purest form was probably
in Stoic and neo-Platonic philosophers of the late classical
and early Christian centuries, and later in the rationalist-
agnostic scientists of the nineteenth century. But it remained an element in Christian philosophy through the
so-called ages of faith and down to our own times, although
it was greatly modified by Christian trinitarianism, which
personalized it and made it religiously concrete and not
merely speculative. Many if not most of the great scientists since the seventeenth century were able to combine
the scientific dogma of universal causality with a faith in
the living God (earth's Creator and man's Redeemer).
But just as polytheism continued in an underground form
through the Middle Ages and lives on today in modern
cults of witchcraft and Satanism, the imagination of Western man was never fully Christianized or even convinced
by abstract monotheism's picture of a universe of law.

Intellectually and culturally polytheism has been un-
fashionable for a long time. Western man does not feel
himself inclined to make graven images. Yet this fact has
done nothing to discourage the idolatrous imagination. It
simply has made polytheism show itself in other forms,
most of them not recognized as such by the idolaters themselves. Almost certainly some remnant of the polytheistic
outlook lives on in each of us. As happened for Israel,
conscious profession of faith in the one God does not
prevent the imagination of men's hearts turning them back
to worship "strange gods." Our own assumption that we
are faithful to the Judeo-Christian tradition of faith may
well be belied in practice as unconscious memories stir
within us, causing us to tremble before the cosmic powers
and endeavor to placate them.

Thus the idolatrous imagination may be buried, but it
is not dead. In the past this imagination led to the making
of graven images. It is not at all impossible that it may do
so again in our own times, given the appropriate psychological and cultural conditions. What is certain is that so
long as men resist opening their hearts to the rule of the
living God, the drive toward idolatry can never cease to be

an inward force that will find an expression appropriate to the times.

John Calvin recognized this truth when he expounded the Ten Commandments in his *Institutes*. He began by writing of the First Commandment, and referring to the Second, in these terms:

> The purport of this commandment is, that the Lord will have himself alone to be exalted in his people, and claims entire possession of them as his own. That it may be so, he orders us to abstain from ungodliness and superstition of every kind, by which the glory of his divinity is diminished or obscured; and, for the same reason, he requires us to worship and adore him with truly pious zeal. For seeing we cannot have God without embracing everything that belongs to him, the prohibition against having strange gods means, that nothing which belongs to him is to be transferred to any other (II, viii, 16).

These words are as appropriate today as they were when written in the sixteenth century. The modern idolatrous imagination still refuses to believe that the promises of the living God are sure and that his grace is sufficient for all our needs. It still looks to other powers and other authorities for support and guidance, transferring to them what belongs to the Creator alone.

3

DISTINGUISHING THE SPIRITS: A TASK FOR TODAY

The Spirit of the Age

We often speak of the "climate" of a culture or the "spirit" of an age. This is a concept not readily pinned down. It is easy to recognize yet hard to define, something sensed rather than demonstrated. The most reliable pointer to this elusive entity is to be found in art. The climate or spirit of the eighteenth century, for example, is epitomized in the works of Mozart and Fragonard and Alexander Pope; that of the nineteenth century in the works of Mendelssohn and Gustave Doré and Alfred Lord Tennyson.

I have argued that what people think they know is less fundamental than the forms of their imagination — the images through which they view the world around them. The leading place of art in allowing us to grasp the spirit of an age supports this thesis. Art is an excellent guide to recognizing the Zeitgeist because the artist works concretely in images. In different periods of history there are images that seem to be especially meaningful to the contemporary imagination. These images are most fully and significantly displayed in the artistic productions of the time. Furthermore, it is often noted that we see the spirit of an age best represented, not in the giants of artistic creativity, but in the lesser figures of the period. This, too, makes sense in light of our thesis. Great artists are frequently ahead of their time and so are judged to be difficult to understand. They bring new images to a public unprepared to take these images into their imaginative picture of the world. Popular artists employ images already familiar and easily interpreted by the contemporary imagination.

Philosophers and theologians, unlike artists, do not work in concrete images. Yet their work also reflects indirectly the dominant images of their time, images drawn both from the art and from the practical concerns of the contemporary culture. Many historians have noted the similarity between Aquinas' massive *Summae,* with their architectonic sense of order and inventive amplitude, and the Gothic cathedral, which also reached its perfection in the thirteenth century. Similarly, the "geometric" reasoning of Descartes and Spinoza shows the impression made on the seventeenth-century imagination by the mathematical advances of the age. Moreover, the conviction of these philosophers that philosophy was drawing an entirely new map of the universe, starting for the first time on sound principles, reminds us that this was the great age of geographical exploration, when men were making maps of a world with vastly different horizons from those imagined in the Middle Ages. Again, Hegel's philosophy of cosmic evolution carries forward the image of mankind's slow but triumphant climb out of ignorance into light, which was the vision of the Enlightenment. This image of the onward and upward movement of history reflects the "historical sense" that had come into eighteenth-century art.[1] At the same time, Hegel's theory of the unity of the divine and the human was imaginatively prepared by the romantic writers, with whom Hegel had close ties, and their vision of creativity as lying within man himself, not a divine gift received from outside. In our own day, British analytical philosophy may have been influenced by the analytical

---

[1] It is interesting that the first true "historical painting" — that is, one attempting to reconstruct an actual moment in history, complete with accurate details of the costume of that time — was John Copley's "The Death of Chatham." Copley was an American, and the New World was considered by the intellectuals of the eighteenth century to be the home of freedom in thought untrammeled by old-world authoritarianism.

method in literary criticism; and both of these movements may well have been suggested by the model of chemical analysis. There certainly seems to be some resemblance between the productions of analytical philosophers and literary critics and the fictional monograph of Sherlock Holmes on the one hundred and forty varieties of tobacco ash!

It might seem fanciful to suggest that a single image, such as the word "analysis," could possibly spark the development of an influential intellectual movement. Yet if we take the power of the imagination seriously, this is no farfetched hypothesis. Given the right circumstances, an image can wield an extraordinary influence. Commercial advertisers know this. They enrich themselves and their clients with informed guesses about attractive images — and not only the obvious pictorial ones like a girl in a bikini. The inclusion of a word or a phrase to which there is a positive "consumer reaction" will achieve surprising results for an advertisement.

This principle operates in every sphere and for every human being, sophisticated or unsophisticated. The ordinary man runs eagerly (for a time) to buy the brand of gasoline that (he is told) will put a tiger in his tank. His reaction is really no different from that of the learned specialist who repeats with conviction the phrases of the latest "authority" in his field while heaping derision upon previous authorities now temporarily out of style. The most highly developed critical intelligence finds it hard to escape the magical attraction of the image that glows brightly in the firmament of the contemporary imagination.

So, while the spirit of an age shows itself most clearly in art, it is carried in the pervasive images of the day through all the forms of cultural expression and at every cultural level. The elusive quality of the Zeitgeist arises largely from the fact that images are not only omnipresent, but also operate at all levels of consciousness. The artist calls them into being in his search for a wider vision of the world. The critic tries to identify and evaluate them. The advertiser and the propagandist manipulate them deliberately for their emotional appeal. The thinker tries to translate them into conceptual terms. But no one can get behind them entirely so as to be able to do without them. Images mediate the world to us. Because we are social beings the images we use to communicate our thoughts, feelings, and intentions reflect the spirit of the age. At the same time, because we are individuals, our own personal way of using images reflects the quality of our imaginations and contributes to the age, affecting it for better or for worse.

Diversities of Spirits

The language of an age is the chief storehouse of its images. Out of this storehouse each generation draws for its particular needs, adding to it as it sees fit and discarding what seems to have served its purpose and is no longer useful.

Language strives to turn images into concepts. Yet in this it never wholly succeeds. Words are always more than signs having precise, intelligible meanings. They remain images, dependent for their significance on the imaginations of those who use them. Thus, although dictionaries are supposed to give the meaning of words, they can do so only by using other words. The consequence is that dictionary meanings are like kittens chasing their own tails. There can be no definitive dictionary definitions, but only an interim report on what a word generally means for the time being. When the next edition of the dictionary is brought out, the definition of that word may have to be altered.

Dictionaries compiled on an historical basis can, by giving dated examples, show us how words have actually been used at different periods of history. They allow us to trace how words have become modified in meaning through the centuries. Changes in the imaginative vision of different generations have sharpened some images and dulled others; so one class of words gains precision while another class becomes more vague and general. Where men's imaginations begin to concentrate upon certain experiences, new words become necessary. Where imaginative interest flags, words drop out of use entirely.[2] Meaning in language is never static, because it is a barometer recording the fluctuations of the cultural climate as the generations pass. Each new generation accepts some and rejects other aspects of the imaginative picture of the world held by its predecessor.

Although language is a common cultural possession for a people and has a common history that can be examined as though it were a single entity, no two individuals use it in the same way. There are many words and combinations of words to choose from, and many subtly different shades of meaning can be given to the words we use. The images that we express in words are given us in part by the "accepted sense" of those words, but in part they are our own. To some extent each one of us is an artist creating verbal images, a poet giving form to this unique imaginative approach to the world. We belong to our age, but we are not bound by it in every respect. We contribute to the common heritage of language in which we participate both by agreeing with it and by rebelling against it, both by using the familiar verbal images that it provides and by modifying them and inventing new ones.

In language usage we are most dependent on the contemporary cultural community. If our words are too individual and reflect too purely personal a vision, we run the risk of not being understood at all. This is an occupational hazard for artists, but the rest of us find a measure of conformity necessary. Nevertheless, language always pro-

[2]The history of a language is not the only evidence for the extent to which imaginative attention dominates human language. The comparative study of languages provides fascinating data documenting the same phenomenon. For example, a tribe that raises cattle will have many words for cows and their care, but perhaps only one word for both sowing and reaping; while for a neighboring agricultural tribe the reverse obtains. See Ernst Cassirer, *Language and Myth* (New York: Harper, 1956), pp 39-40. Cassirer's work traces how conceptualization arises out of mythological images. It has helped me formulate my own ideas on language and the imagination.

vides a large field in which personal imagination can take its distinctive and individual path. Widely diverse and conflicting pictures of the world can and do coexist in every generation; even though some are far more influential than others. In the matter of the conceptual interpretation of images, certainly, there are always a number of hotly contested options. No generation is free from conflicts over ideologies.

So we can speak of the spirit of an age with assurance only by looking backward on some period in the past and picking out the most prominent images to be found in its cultural productions: its art and literature, its philosophies and theologies, its artifacts, its social organizations and customs, its political parties, and its religious cults. Even then we generalize broadly, knowing that we are excluding a great deal that cannot be pressed into the mold of our generalizations. If we try to identify the spirit of the present age, plausible generalization becomes infinitely harder. We lack the perspective to distinguish between passing fashions and continuing trends. There are so many voices raised around us that it is almost impossible to sort out those which are influential from those which are simply loud.

Many-voiced our present culture unquestionably is. Indeed, there are those who would argue that it is in a state of dissolution, rapidly being torn apart by the upsurge of various countercultures. Perhaps a century from now historians will be able to point out how the fury of the conflicts between diverse spirits was itself part of the ruling spirit of our age. After all, every age carries within it a diversity of spirits; though in some periods of history the opposition between them is hardly visible, while at other periods it breaks through for all to see.

I shall not try to anticipate the judgment of the future, except to suggest that our age may be less exceptional than many would have us believe.[3] My purpose in this excursus

---

[3]Later we shall look at the widespread image of the present age as wholly new and unprecedented, and give some reasons for questioning the accuracy of this image. See below, pp. 89-93, 101-02, 135-38.

on language and the diversity of cultural "spirits" is to lay the foundation for the following sections of this book, where I evaluate some of the present tendencies in image-making. The images we use constantly require scrutiny since they bear on our beliefs and may lead us into idolatry. I grant that we are too much caught up in the cross-currents of the many winds of change blowing over our world to be able to speculate about the overall climate of our age. Nevertheless, I think that it is possible to say something about just how some of these winds are catching us at the moment. If there is a Babel of voices around us, we can surely hear whether a number of them are saying the same thing; and we can then ask how this unanimity has come about.

The Significance of the Stock Response

Asking about the "how" of contemporary opinions is actually more important than asking about the "what." Since the perennial springs of idolatry lie in the imaginations of men's hearts, it is not so much individual opinions that matter (though, of course, they do matter greatly) as the imaginative attitude informing these opinions. Often the plain sense, the surface meaning, of the words a person uses does not convey the full import of what he is saying. In order to understand him properly we should also have access to the picture of the universe that gives force to every opinion he expresses. Insight into this more comprehensive meaning must come from how he states his thoughts. "For the words that the mouth utters come from the overflowing of the heart" (Matt. 12:34). The inclination of the heart may not be obvious from the words uttered, but it will be there.

The fact that the surface meaning of words is never the complete meaning is plain from the fact that the spoken word is always much richer than the written word. To listen to someone speaking is to catch more of the "spirit" of the speaker than bare words on a page can convey. Yet the written word also is able to communicate a great deal more than the surface meaning, since language is always imagery as well as meaningful sign. We simply have to use imagination in addition to intelligence when we read.

One clue to the inner sense of words is the evidence that may be found in them of the stock response. The term "stock response" originated in literary criticism, where it was used to indicate an absence of imaginative sensibility and a low level of perception in regard to poetic imagery. Although it refers to the reaction of readers, it could as well be used to pinpoint inadequacies in writers. The contention is as follows. A poor poet lacks the power to make a new image that requires the reader to be alert to the precise imagery contained in the lines before him. So he simply counts on a stock response — an almost automatic reflex — on the part of the reader to make a well-worn image acceptable. The reader who reacts by making that stock response neither wants nor appreciates an unfamiliar image. He will not make the imaginative effort required to look at the world and see there what is to be seen with the help of the right image. Instead, he is happy to be reassured that any such effort is unnecessary. Believing that his image of reality is the right one — indeed, the only sensible one — he simply asks that his knowledge be confirmed through the repetition by others of an image that he himself uses. To this kind of prostitution of imagery by the reader the bad writer panders.

The stock response is not limited to literature. It is found wherever the imagination is called into play, that is, wherever men act, judge, or think. A prime example of the image used to obtain a stock response is seen in the insulting names used by the racist bigot. *Kike, wop, Polack, nigger* — when these names are applied to other persons, their individuality and humanity disappear behind a general image of contempt. The actuality disappears. The image alone remains, reinforcing the complacent Pharisaism of the bigot, reassuring him that *he is not as other men* and shutting out any contact with reality that threat-

ens his complacency. The image is really the only weapon
he has to protect his imagination against truths he dare
not acknowledge. For that reason, he delights in every
occasion when the use of the image demonstrates its
power to hurt those against whom it is directed and to
rally those of like imagination to his own.

This example of the stock response is extreme in one
respect: it exhibits moral as well as imaginative deficiency.
There is nothing absolutely sinister about a stock response
as such. It need not necessarily be mistaken; indeed, under
certain circumstances it may even be adequate. Yet the
myopia of its imaginative vision is a danger signal. Again,
the "how" counts for more than the "what." The stock
response may or may not indicate false opinions; but it
always indicates indifference to the possibility that one's
opinions may have to be revised, or that there are more
things in heaven and earth than are imaged in one's present imagination. Peril lies in the complacent attitude
which, if persisted in, can lead to complete insulation
from living reality. Imaginative myopia then deteriorates
into unsuspected blindness. "Some Pharisees in his company asked, 'Do you mean that we are blind?' 'If you
were blind,' said Jesus, 'you would not be guilty, but
because you say *We see* your guilt remains" (John 9:
40-41).

The stock response demands — and feeds on — clichés,
slogans, and catchwords. These three birds of a feather
frequently flock together.[4] And who can do without
them? Clichés, in particular, are almost a necessity; and
a complete embargo on their use would almost certainly
mean the end of human communication. Frail humanity
needs such helpful crutches to support the legs of its
imagination, which cannot walk for long unaided in the

[4]Proverbs, too, are occasions of the stock response. Originally, a proverb
was meant to encapsulate the wisdom of mature experience and thus to
encourage breadth of vision. The Book of Proverbs speaks of men gaining
"well-instructed intelligence, righteousness, justice, and probity" through
interpreting "the sayings of wise men and their riddles" (Prov. 1:2-6). But
today proverbs are more often a substitute for wisdom than an incentive
to it.

kingdom of images. If we apply the principle of "how rather than what" we will moderate the harshness with which we judge the cliché. It is cliché-mongering rather than the cliché itself that is hurtful. Indeed — paradoxically — there can be a stock response to clichés. People affecting an intense disgust for clichés often exhibit this. Failing to distinguish between use and abuse, they also neglect the partial truth that a cliché may contain because of their scorn for the container.

Slogans and catchwords are not usually as harmless as clichés. To the element of constant repetition that is supposed to prove the cliché's truth, the slogan and catchword add an element of emotional persuasion sometimes amounting almost to blackmail. Both clichés and slogans state supposedly self-evident truths, unproven but counting upon a stock response to uphold them. The slogan, however, is a kind of would-be cliché. The hour of triumph when it can count upon an almost universal stock response has not yet arrived; and so it works harder. Clichés we can take or leave. Slogans are thrown at us.

While a slogan can elicit a genuine stock response only when it has become familiar enough to stand by itself, it requires a preliminary backing from indoctrinating propaganda.[5] No one really asks to see a formal justification for clichés like "Honesty is the best policy" or "Things will look better in the morning." On the other hand, "Never trust anyone over thirty" and "The medium is the message" are slogans demanding elaboration in some specific theory. Commercial slogans are judged successful to the extent that supporting information becomes unnecessary, and the slogan does it all. "Druggets are the dependable sleeping pills, because they contain seventeen scientifically tested ingredients. And only Druggets give you the peppermint flavor to bring new freshness into your dreams. Remember, *Druggets drop you into Dreamland.*" When people who wish to express the state of

---

[5]Since the stock response to the words "propaganda" and "indoctrination" is negative, the preferred phrase is in-depth instruction. Ask any encyclopedia salesman.

tranquility in general, start quoting the last five words of this advertisement, the slogan has arrived. It could not have done so at a time when no one had heard of Drug-gets or knew what they were. Nor is any kind of slogan different in this respect from the commercial slogan. It requires vigorous promotion.

Catchwords are slogans in miniature, achieving through their extreme concentration of an image a maximum emotional impact. The racial nickname already referred to is one type of catchword. Catchwords are perhaps the most effective stimulants of the stock response.[6]

Together, contemporary clichés, slogans and catchwords provide important evidence concerning the way in which men's imaginations are being influenced. Here, if anywhere, it is possible to gain insight into the "spirits" current in the present age.

True Spirits and False

The early Christian church gave recognition to those gifted by the Holy Spirit with the "ability to distinguish true spirits from false" (I Cor. 12:10). Some of the "spirits" requiring to be distinguished are present, as in every age, within the contemporary culture.

During the first Christian century we have evidence for this in the New Testament itself. The faithful are warned:

> Do not trust any and every spirit, my friends; test the spirits, to see whether they are from God, for among those who have gone out into the world there are many prophets falsely inspired. This is how we may recognize the Spirit of God: every spirit which acknowledges that Jesus Christ has come in the flesh is from God, and every spirit which does not thus acknowledge Jesus is not from God (I John 4:1-3).

The letter goes on to affirm that the false prophets belong to "the godless world," while the church is guided by

---

[6]In Part Two we shall be looking more closely at the power of the catch-word over the imagination. See below, pp. 66-69.

God; and so those who refuse the church's message belong to the world. "That is how we distinguish the spirit of truth from the spirit of error" (I John 4:4-6).

It would seem that the First Letter of John is speaking of the existence within the Christian community of a fairly fully developed form of the Gnosticism that Paul encountered in a much milder form at Corinth. The Gnostic Christians' "knowledge" went so far as to deny that Christ has come in the flesh. This denial originated in the fact that the picture of the world imagined by the Gnostics was one that made an absolute separation between the "spiritual" and the "material." Thus John affirms that the distinction between true and false spirits was to be found in whether the imagination of the Gnostics determined what the Christian message was to be or whether the apostolic witness to Jesus Christ was to be followed (I John 1:1-4).

It is surely not accidental that the First Letter of John should end with a warning against idols (I John 5:21). Nowhere else in the letter are pagan idols mentioned, so that this final sentence seems to sum up the condemnation of Gnostic teaching that is so prominent there. If that indeed is the meaning intended, our use of the term "the idolatrous imagination" finds direct support in the New Testament.[7]

In our survey of the connection between idolatry and the imagination, a persistent theme has been the opposition between the historical revelation given in Scripture and the claim to possess "knowledge" independently of revelation. The scriptural judgment on all such "knowledge" is that it is quite other than the wisdom having its source in the living God. Rather than being divine truth, it is nothing else than "the imagination of men's hearts." Very much in keeping with the development of this theme elsewhere in the Bible, I John precedes the warning against idols

---

[7]Not all commentators agree that Gnostic heresies rather than pagan images are intended here by the word "idols," but a great many do. See *Words and the Word*, p. 71 and footnote. The Jerusalem Bible appends a note to I John 5:21, mentioning the phrase "idols of the heart" found in the Qumran Scrolls. Thus the usage was a current one.

with a stress on the contrast between false gods and the one true God, from whom all truth comes. John writes:

> We know that the Son of God has come and given us under-standing to know him who is real; indeed we are in him who is real, since we are in his Son Jesus Christ. This is the true God, this is eternal life. My children, be on the watch against false gods [*eidoloi*, idols] (I John 5:20-21).

First John then, as well as I Corinthians, stresses the connection between idolatry and all knowledge confident of possessing the truth yet ignorant of the truth of the living God. Idolatry is more than image-worship, since it is essentially the absence of loving obedience to the God who has revealed himself beyond anything that we could dare to believe. Contempt of image-worshipers, therefore, is in itself no break with idolatry so long as it continues to manufacture its own image of the divine, glorying not in the living God but in its own self-image. It follows that distinguishing between true and false spirits in the church has to do with the contrast between being *in the truth* revealed by God in Jesus Christ — the truth *known in him* — and claiming to *have the truth in ourselves*. Imagining that the truth lies within our own spirit — and will rise up at our command — means that we, no less than the image-maker, bow down before what we ourselves have made. For our imagination is our interior workshop. The Christian gospel knows only the living Word who is the Truth, sent from the Father (John 14:6), and living now in the believer through the indwelling of the Spirit of truth (John 14:17).

The opening chapter focussed on how Scripture bases all genuine knowledge of the truth on the personal self-com-munication of God. The second chapter commented on the knowledge-claims of the demythologizers, which actu-ally do not rest on knowledge at all, but on imaginative constructions. In the present chapter we have been look-ing at the effects of the working of the imagination in raising up different forms of "spirits." And, in the mech-anism of the stock response, we have seen one possible human vehicle for transmitting "the spirit of this world," which claims the possession of perfect knowledge and final truth.

In Part Two further examination will be made of the working of the stock response in our age. The stock response lies at the base of much present-day ideological thinking — this kind of thinking being the *imaging* that creates the contemporary face of idolatry.

It would seem that idolatry has not changed much over the centuries, except that it has discarded its more blatant forms for something a little more subtle. Chiefly, the external image has given place to the internal one. Yet the idolater still maintains his distinctive stance. Seen from the biblical perspective, he continues to be the blind man who says that he sees. He blindly denies the living God, asserting that he can see clearly the foolishness of faith in such a deity. This God of revelation, he complains, is not a god at all. At one time the complaint is raised that a real god must have a visible image; and the God of Israel has none. At another time the complaint states that a real god must be conceived abstractly as the Unconditional; and the God and Father of our Lord Jesus Christ is an anthropomorphic conception, and so unbelievable. The forms of the imaginations of men's hearts change, but the content remains constant. At Babel man believed he could construct a tower reaching to heaven. Today he is proud of having discovered that heaven is not "up there." He is sure that the myth of reaching heaven means looking within to plumb the depths of the human spirit; and to reach these depths, he believes, is most certainly within his power.

Within our age, as within every other, the worship of the one God in the spirit of obedient faith is tempted to be drawn astray by the spirit of idolatry. Today, as at all times during mankind's history, there is a task to be undertaken by the church of Jesus Christ. It is the task of distinguishing between the spirit of truth and the spirit of error, so that she may never cease to turn from idols and serve the living God.

Part Two

IDOLS OF THE MODERN MARKET-PLACE

4

THE CULT OF RELEVANCE

The argument so far has intended to show that idolatry cannot be limited to particular periods in human history or to particular developments in human culture, and that it certainly is not a phenomenon of former ages that has now vanished from the scene. Because idolatry is a product of "the imagination of men's hearts," it is always with us. The forms taken by the idolatrous imagination are constantly changing; the thing itself remains and finds ever new expressions. In the present chapter and the two following we shall examine some of the expressions of idolatry in our own times and the idols set up to be worshiped in the market-places where "images" are manufactured for our modern technological culture. That these images are mental rather than visible representations of divine beings does not make them the less actual as strange gods proposed as alternatives to the living God.

Artifacts as Images

There is one theme that runs throughout our whole argument: the extent to which conscious thinking is given its direction by the images present in the imagination. Though often totally unrecognized or barely suspected, these images carry immense power. The way man's thinking goes — and thus the way his life goes — is intimately connected with the quality of his imagination.

The quality of man's imagination finds expression through the images he makes, whether these images are material or spiritual. In the preceding chapter I referred to how the spirit of an age is always most readily identified by the art that the age produces, since artists deal directly in images. But human artifacts of every kind give valuable evidence of the spirit of an age. This is because they are pieces of applied art. Archaeologists use the shape and decoration of pots, for example, to date the different periods of culture in an early civilization and to estimate how "advanced" a culture might have been.

As art objects, artifacts have symbolic value as well as supplying us with information about the history of culture. The roads and viaducts built by the Romans wherever they occupied a territory provide us with visible images of the organizing skill and will-to-power of the Roman Empire. These utilitarian works exemplify "the grandeur that was Rome" as much as, if not more than, the triumphal arches and portrait busts.

Since the seventeenth century, however, the rise of the scientific spirit, with its new aspiration to subdue and control nature through exact knowledge, has created a special type of human artifact — the machine. Like the rest of man's handiwork, machines are symbols as well as useful objects. In the seventeenth century the clock had a special symbolic importance. When the men of that age constructed accurate clocks that were used as scientific instruments and not mere social conveniences, they became well aware of their symbolic significance. The clock mirrored the regular laws of the universe. This regularity so impressed the seventeenth-century mind that God himself was called the Great Clock-maker. By the eighteenth century, the imaginative vision of a clocklike universe had been applied to man. The French doctor La Mettrie, in his tract *L'Homme Machine,* claimed to describe "the various springs that move the human machine."

Although the power of steam had been known for centuries, it was not until the 1800s that steam was harnessed to be man's efficient servant. The steam locomotive became the most potent symbol of nineteenth-century civilization. In the twentieth century, with the invention of the internal combustion engine, the automobile took its place as the leading symbol of the times.

At first glance it seems paradoxical that the steam locomotive, a communal means of transport, should have become the symbol of an age known for its "rugged individualism," whereas the private car images our own age of collectivism and mass communications. Yet on closer inspection the paradox disappears. The nineteenth-century belief in private enterprise meant accepting the will of a dominating employer as expressive of men's ability to conquer the environment and make it bring forth wealth. The powerful locomotive, pulling passive, consenting passengers and loaded freight cars, was a perfect image of the powerful industrialist's role in society. The railroad kings laid bands of steel over the whole land, binding the wilderness into the body of industrial America.[1]

The image of the steam locomotive found its conceptual expression in the belief in inevitable progress through evolution. The popular Darwinian philosophy that is expressed in T. H. Huxley's slogan "the survival of the fittest" was applied to the free-enterprise system, which could not be interfered with, since the "natural" evolution of society demanded that the "natural" leaders prove themselves by eliminating weaker competitors. Just as steam power ruled in the world of industry, so energy of will power ruled among the controllers of that world. The strongest and

---

[1] It is interesting that in our own age this symbol is not quite dead. When Ayn Rand wished to prove in her novel *Atlas Shrugged* that the nineteenth-century philosophy of free enterprise was the only viable one for any free society, she chose as the central character the daughter of one of these railroad kings. The action of the novel centers around the effort of this iron-willed woman to keep a railroad operating in spite of the efforts of a band of collectivist pirates to sabotage it.

most capable hands on the controls of the locomotive of technological progress were considered essential for keeping it moving along the track.

The Automobile: A Contemporary Image

With the coming of the automobile this image changed to one of many vehicles, each with its own driver democratically sharing the highway, as he followed the route to a destination that he himself had chosen. No longer did the iron law of the railroad demand the driver to keep on the track. He could branch off when he wished. He was obedient to no fixed timetable. Automobiles served the convenience of their owners. The traveler could still take public transport if he wished, but increasingly he did not, and so public transport withered. The Victorian ethic, which demanded rigid standards for all, withered likewise: the new ideal was "do your own thing." Actual power to control others was not so important as the sensation of power given by speed. The ability to pass others and leave them behind was what really counted. And, very soon, the automobile was valued for its being available to take its owner away from the world of competitive struggle and productivity, to leave it all behind. Whereas the locomotive had tamed the wilderness and brought it into civilization, the automobile took individuals who were weary of civilization into the few remaining corners of the wilderness that had not been (as it was now thought) spoiled.

Nevertheless, the freedom brought by the automobile was much less than promised. If all wanted to be car owners, all had to learn to want (within narrow limits) the same kind of car. Tastes had to be standardized to fit the assembly line. The freedom of the road became, during most driving hours, the freedom to move in lines almost as rigid as assembly lines. There was no release from the rule of law; instead, the ordinary citizen was more than ever before in contact with the police. To meet the collective needs of motorists, highways and the urban sprawl accompanying them spoiled the countryside on a scale far exceeding anything the railroads had done; while automobile fumes became a major pollutant of the air. Most of all, in an age that looked back with horror at the disregard for human life shown in earlier ages, the yearly sum of deaths and maimings on the roads exceeded most of those caused by war and famine in the past.

No previous conqueror changed the external face of the world so drastically. It is no wonder that the automobile has also changed modern man's imaginative picture of his world. It has brought him to expect that what he thinks important when he chooses his car must be the touchstone of value universally.

Some psychologists suggest that the male car owner thinks of his vehicle as a mistress. That may be fanciful. But the pairing of the supposedly desirable automobile and the supposedly desirable woman in automobile advertisements is almost universal. No doubt men are thereby encouraged to think of the ideal woman in terms of the machine. She should be young (a late model), vivacious (racy), sensitive to male moods (responsive on the road), desirable (the envy of other drivers), and disposable (easily traded in if she shows signs of giving trouble).

Yet such an obvious image, though influential, is not as important in the long run as others more hidden. Many who reject the particular car-image described above tacitly accept a transposition of the same image. Some advocates of women's liberation, for instance, strongly repudiate the image of woman as a "use object." At the same time, their own way of speaking strongly suggests the image of the liberated woman as a driver and her career as a car. In this picture, the reason why women have such difficulty competing with men is that the authorities are specifically male, all intent upon keeping the road to themselves. Male legislators draw up the highway code of social custom and male police enforce it. (The common image of a "pig," used both for the police and the male opposed to the ideals of women's liberation, is informative in this context.)

The ideal of liberation itself, irrespective of sexual

distinctions, may well owe much to the automobile as a symbol of modern living. When the driver heads down an open road for a weekend away from the city, he has an image of himself as a free spirit. The only obstacles to complete freedom are external ones: speed zones, bad roads, detours, engine trouble, and the authoritarian interference of police. If this particular image is applied to society at large, it would seem to follow that the road to the good life would be quick indeed if hampering external conditions were removed. It is the System, existing "structures," and the continued enforcement of out-of-date laws designed (as the instructive common phrase has it) for *horse-and-buggy days* that alone hold us back. Social engineering to usher in the perfect society ought to be as straightforward a task as building adequate roads for today's traffic. A sober view of the situation, of course, would have to face the fact that all efforts to solve traffic problems by building more and wider and faster highways have only made them seem insoluble without banning the automobile altogether. But such realism is hardly to be expected at the moment, since few people can imagine an existence without cars. When we complain about the impossible conditions of driving, it is always the other cars we are complaining about. Somehow, we know that we ourselves unquestionably have a right to be there.

I am not suggesting that the automobile is the one and only image underlying contemporary thinking. But ever since the seventeenth century there has been an evident tendency to picture the world in terms of man's technological achievements. The automobile is one prominent example of these achievements in our own age, and an especially familiar one since it influences so much of everyone's day-to-day living. In some ways the airplane is a more spectacular symbol of our age. Many people are characterizing the second half of the twentieth century as "the space age" or "the age of the computer." While these more recent products of technology certainly do enter into our consciousness and provide new terms for our vocabulary (for example, tailspin, feedback, countdown), none of them touches the life of the ordinary individual so closely, or affects his life-style in so many ways, as the automobile. When we draw on a less familiar technological object as a source for our images, we are more likely to be conscious of what we are doing and to remember that we are dealing with an analogy, which is not to be applied uncritically. It is always the extremely familiar image that slips unnoticed into our minds and is used by our imaginations as an unexamined interpretive key to all experience. And as a symbol on this level the automobile occupies a place by itself.

Consider, for example, the following statement about Christianity in the world today:

> Traditional Christianity is largely irrelevant to the current world situation. For any religion to become and remain a vital force in the lives of a new generation it must be remodeled from time to time. This is especially important in times of rapid and basic social change. Ours are such times, and Christianity has not kept pace.[2]

The argument here hinges on the assertion that religion has to be *remodeled* from time to time. When the writer says that, he is using an image taken from the automobile industry — which has no very clear connection with the history of religions. Indeed, no evidence is offered that has anything to do with religion. The assumption is that religion, like everything else worthy of the attention of men today, *must* follow the pattern of industrial production. It must "keep pace" with the market and meet the demand of consumers, who will most definitely demand the latest model off the assembly line. Who would drive a car that could not "keep pace" with the traffic on today's turnpikes? And is not the "current world situation" to be thought of in terms of driving along a high-speed highway?

The Catchword "Relevance"

The statement noted above concerning the irrelevance

[2]Gustave Todrank, *The Secular Search for a New Christ* (Philadelphia: Westminster, 1969), p. 7.

of traditional Christianity leads directly to the subject of this chapter, the catchword "relevance." That statement is representative of numerous statements made in recent years about "the contemporary religious situation." It advances sentiments we have all seen, expressed in almost identical terms, dozens (if not hundreds) of times.

It may be useful to begin by saying something about catchwords and their dependence on the stock response. We spoke earlier about the stock response and the evidence that this personal reaction provides about the quality of the imagination of those who give it or seek to elicit it.[3] A person gives a stock response when he understands words, but does not deliberately reflect on them. Instead, an immediate emotional reaction — positive or negative — ensues. A stock response is elicited when words are used with the intent to obtain such an unthinking reaction. We mentioned clichés, slogans, and catchwords as three common forms of verbal expression parasitic on the stock response. Of these the catchword is the most concentrated. By means of a single word or short phrase the imagination can be triggered to react predictably — and frequently explosively.

The word "catchword" originally referred to the printing of the first word on a page as the foot of the preceding page, so that it would catch the eye of the assembler when the book was put together. It was later used for any word prominently placed on a page. It has since come to mean any word that has caught the popular mind. In other words, it is a word that catches the intelligence and holds it captive in a net of prejudice. Once a catchword ceases to be popular, it becomes a common object for ridicule. Its emotional impact, in effect, acts in reverse. So today many people refer with contempt to those politicians who appeal to motherhood and the flag in order to conceal lack of principle. The lifespan of a catchword is always limited. Yet so long as it retains its hold over the contemporary, one challenges it at his peril.

[3]See above, pp. 48-52.

"Relevance" is such a catchword. According to today's stock reaction, anything labeled relevant is above criticism, and anything labeled irrelevant is beneath contempt. The affirmation of the supreme worth of relevance becomes an article of faith, and the pursuit of relevance a cult.

Thus relevance has become to a large extent today's criterion of value. It certainly outranks goodness. If someone says, "This seems good to me," someone else will almost certainly say, "Yes, perhaps. But is it relevant?" No longer is it enough to prove worth unless relevance also can be claimed; by the same token, if relevance is granted, the notion of worth is not even taken into account. In the late sixties there was vociferous and tumultuous agitation within universities to overhaul the curriculum and make it relevant. It was not argued that subjects be taught because they promoted intellectual agility and enlarged our mental horizons, and decidedly not that any subject had proved itself through the years to be a fit component of university education. The criterion was relevance, which in fact meant immediate attractiveness. The appeal was to the imagination current at that time, under the assumption that imaginative horizons of the moment were the widest possible ones and that the contemporary consciousness had suddenly come into contact with a fulness of truth never before perceived. A new generation had come on the scene, possessing an insight into their times that no one belonging to the previous generation could possibly share.

It was in this period also that "social change" became a companion catchword to "relevance." Rapid social change was upon us. To work for social change meant to be committed to the highest value. No one even considered that social change might as easily be for the worse as for the better. One was either for change or for its diabolical spiritual enemy, the status quo. Moreover, since the status quo maintained its malignant powers through the established structures of traditional institutions (personified as "the Establishment") and through the inertia of traditional attitudes, *tradition* became the focal point at which all the forces inimical to social change declared themselves. In every appeal to tradition was to be seen the very essence of the irrelevant.

A characteristic of catchwords is that they tend to gather in families, in which each supports the other in eliciting a stock response. Let us look again at the passage we cited earlier:

> Traditional Christianity is largely irrelevant to the current world situation. For any religion to become and remain a vital force in the lives of a new generation it must be remodeled from time to time. This is especially important in times of rapid and basic social change. Ours are such times, and Christianity has not kept pace.

It is evident that this whole statement depends for its effect on a stock response to catchwords. The only part of it that puts forward any argument is the part that (as we pointed out) depends on the dubious hidden analogy between religion and the automobile. The rest simply states what are assumed to be facts because catchwords make them so.

For example, why are we supposed to agree that traditional Christianity is largely irrelevant to the current world situation? If the presence of "rapid and basic social change" is the answer, it is surely *relevant* that traditional Christianity survived the breakdown of the Roman Empire, the passing of the Dark Ages into the Middle Ages, the transition between the Middle Ages and the Renaissance, the skepticism of the Enlightenment and the overthrow of absolutist monarchies, and the change through the Industrial Revolution of an agrarian civilization into an urbanized one. Granted that there were many violent upheavals in the process, the continuity of tradition throughout is as remarkable as are the drastic changes of form that tradition underwent down the centuries. The greatest of these changes, the Reformation, was specifically a movement to recover traditional Christianity and restore it to purity. It would seem that, instead of any attempt to examine evidence, the statement of traditional Christianity's irrelevance simply counts on a stock response to the word "traditional." Nothing traditional can be relevant. A new generation has arrived and has, with its infallible intuitive power of recognizing the irrelevant, pronounced on everything that comes down from previous generations the verdict: "Hasn't kept pace."

Unanswered, of course, is the question of what keeping pace actually entails. And the strong presumption is that no such question has ever even been raised. "Irrelevance" is, by unspoken definition, that which "has not kept pace." What "has not kept pace" is everything that carries the label "traditional." The label "traditional" guarantees "irrelevance." And so on, around and around. Clearly, what we are being given is a statement of a position, resting on the cumulative effect of producing several catchwords belonging to one family. We have not seen any logical argument for this position.

The Irrelevance of Relevance

The blanket statement "This is irrelevant" is irrelevant to all rational discourse. In the world we live in nothing can be finally irrelevant. To deny this would be to contradict ourselves. Suppose we make the assertion that X is irrelevant. This assertion must itself be relevant; yet we cannot make it without mentioning X. Then X, too, is proven relevant. (This argument, incidentally, is simply a variant of Augustine's argument against universal skepticism.) Anything whatever that *is* in any sense — that is, anything imaginable — is relevant to everything else that is. Thus, simply to speak of relevance is to say nothing more than that we are speaking about something in connection with something else — which is the condition of all speech. If speech is to be informative, we must assert why we believe something to stand in a certain relation to something else. That is, we must make a truth claim. The same holds good when we speak of irrelevance. In calling anything irrelevant we are denying a specific relationship, and we must make clear what relationship we have in mind and give reasons for our denial. Again, the issue of truth has to be faced.

Theoretically, everything is relevant to everything else.

This truth is illustrated in the old saying that one cannot move a single pebble on the beach without affecting the entire universe. We grant the point in effect when we speak about the *uni*verse. But practically, we recognize degrees of relevance. The hunter moves through a total landscape and picks out small indications relevant to tracking his quarry. The historian examines documents and selects what is relevant to the subject of his research. Such activities show, in Aristotelian terms, the use of practical reason.

In the arena of practical reason, the judge of what is relevant is the man of practical wisdom; and his judgment is relative to his field of specialization. So relevance can never be established *a priori*. In some areas — in courtroom procedure, for instance — rules for determining relevance can be laid down. Yet even here there can be no finality. Those who have followed the Perry Mason TV series know very well how often it is precisely the question objected to by Hamilton Burger as "immaterial, irrelevant, and incompetent" that secures the triumph of justice.

So an undefined appeal to relevance says nothing at all. But if we speak of the irrelevance of relevance, we ought also to bring out the other side and admit the relevance of irrelevance. Man has achieved nearly every advance in his knowledge by bringing into relation things apparently unrelated, that is, by showing the irrelevant to be relevant. The history of science is full of examples of the relevance of the irrelevant. Sir Isaac Newton discovered the relevance of the fall of an apple to the orbits of the planets. Samuel Pepys records that Charles II "laughed mightily" on learning that the members of the Royal Society had done nothing from the time of its founding until his visit except to attempt to weigh air. However, the Merry Monarch did not have the last laugh, since this seemingly absurd and irrelevant activity was to revolutionize the world. Because preconceived ideas of relevance are fatal to the progress of knowledge, Einstein said that the most valuable asset for a scientist is imagination.

Today, because we live in a technological society made possible by scientific research, scientists are no longer scoffed at. Their work is widely considered to be without question the touchstone of relevance. Poetry, on the other hand, is usually considered an irrelevant and decorative luxury. But the poets are the shapers of our language, and language in the last resort controls the direction of our ideas. Poetic images bring together widely separated ranges of experience into an imaginative unity. Where poetry is neglected, imagination atrophies and the vision of the universe becomes narrow and poor.

Undoubtedly, the popularity of the catchword "relevance" is a symptom of that kind of impoverishment. And also it has contributed more than a little to the increase of polarized opinion and so of violence. It is not a great step, psychologically speaking, from judging that another man's beliefs are irrelevant to thinking that his continued existence is unnecessary. Asserting for ourselves the unqualified right to decide what is relevant and assuming that there can be no argument about it indicates a failure in imagination. And it indicates an even greater failure in imaginative sympathy. For it is to deny to others the right to live within the same universe with us unless they think precisely as we do.

Not every appeal to relevance, of course, invokes the full logic of its presupposition. Yet to dismiss anyone's beliefs as irrelevant without precisely specifying the criterion of relevance used is to enter the dangerous territory of arbitrary judgment. And the territory is no less dangerous if it is entered chiefly because many people have gone there first and it seems to be the "in" place to be. The road is also worn smooth by the feet of silly sheep, each following the one in front of it. The fact that we are urged to seek relevance rather than truth makes conformity a virtue, since the bogey of irrelevance that is waved in our faces is clearly the balloon of social unpopularity inflated to fearsome size. How terrible to be left behind while the rest of the crowd streams by! Who would be so bold in such a predicament as to ask where everyone is actually going, or why?

More than a hundred years ago Søren Kierkegaard warned that the age of the crowd was upon us. In such an age, said Kierkegaard, people do not think of deciding for themselves. They follow the advice given to children going off to a party, "Look and see what the others are doing and behave like them."[4] Kierkegaard did not foresee that the process could be so easily helped along by the spread of the catchword "relevance." He did note, however, that the authority that the man-in-the-crowd would willingly obey would be what he termed "the abstract coercion" arising from the spirit of the crowd itself. He understood the power of the stock response over a generation whose imaginations were not alert to the concrete significance of the images they used. When he called the age of the crowd the age of advertising and publicity, he indicated the coming of the state of mind that would respond to catchwords rather than undertake the exacting search for truth.

Contemporary Man — an Abstraction

Kierkegaard explains how the age of the crowd elevates an abstraction called the public as the arbiter of truth, and thus shrugs off the responsibility that each concrete individual ought to take on himself. He writes:

> A public is everything and nothing, the most dangerous of all powers and the most insignificant: one can speak to a whole nation in the name of the public, and still the public will be less than a single real man, however unimportant . . . but the public is also a gruesome abstraction through which the individual will receive his religious formation — or sink.[5]

Kierkegaard stressed the term "the public" because he considered the power of the popular press of his day the chief instrument for encouraging the stock response as a substitute for rational and responsible thinking on the part

---

[4]David Riesman has confirmed Kierkegaard's prophecy in his diagnosis of man today as commonly "other-directed" — gaining his standards by gauging the behavior of those about him — in contrast to nineteenth-century man, who was conspicuously "inner-directed." See *The Lonely Crowd* (New Haven: Yale U.P., 1950).

[5]*The Present Age: and The Difference Between a Genius and an Apostle* (New York: Harper, 1962), pp. 63-64.

of individuals. "The public" was the abstract image used by journalists on which to project their own opinions and thus create the illusion that these were something far more important and universal. Projected as "what the public thinks" and "what the public demands," private prejudice could masquerade as the very *spirit of the age*, the irresistible upsurge of the collective consciousness of a generation. *Vox populi, vox dei.*[6]

The public is by no means the only abstract entity created by the imagination that lives by stock responses and exploited by those who speak or write in order to elicit the stock response. But Kierkegaard performed a useful service in recognizing this entity and in pointing out how it is essentially an abstraction that has been severed from concrete reality. Abstract images or stereotypes are what stock

[6]Kierkegaard had personal reasons for his bitterness toward journalists, because he had suffered from a journalistic campaign that had successfully fixed on him the "image" of an eccentric and a fool. Commenting on newspaper agitation to have the masses "shot down," he once wrote: "God knows that I am not bloodthirsty and I think I have in a terrible degree a sense of my responsibility to God; but nevertheless, I should be ready to take the responsibility upon me, in God's name, of giving the order to fire if I could first of all make absolutely and conscientiously sure that there was not a single man standing in front of the rifles, not a single creature who was not — a journalist" (*The Journals of Soren Kierkegaard, A Selection,* edited by Alexander Dru; London: Oxford, 1938, no. 886).

Kierkegaard's view of "the power of the press" may have been one-sided, but that his fear of its ability to mislead people in the name of "the public" is confirmed for our own day in Christopher Booker's *The Neophiliacs: A Study of the Revolution in English Life in the Fifties and Sixties* (London: Collins, 1969). Drawing his material very largely from newspapers and magazines, Booker shows how the "fantasy" of a few individuals became magnified into a movement that actually brought about a revolution in the cultural consciousness of the British people. Cultural revolution had widespread repercussions in the artistic, moral, social, and political life of the nation. While Booker perhaps tries to prove too much and oversimplifies the complex factors involved in the "revolution," he documents most thoroughly the part played by journalists, both professional and amateur, in conditioning a whole nation to accept an artificially manufactured image of itself. Although he does not use the term "stock response," Booker leaves us in no doubt that slogans and catchwords were the chief mechanisms used, first to create the illusion of "public opinion," and then to exploit what had been created. Booker gives instance after instance of the constant reiteration of loaded words and phrases calculated to make readers accept as incontrovertible fact opinions that had no foundation in reality.

responses respond to. As has been previously indicated, a stock response issues from an imagination of poor quality that accepts images uncritically on the strength of their being familiar and without regard to their being accurately formed or true to reality.[7]

Catchwords are usually successful in direct proportion to their degree of abstraction, and therefore to their usefulness for substituting ideological generalities for precise information about the actual world. If an individual is called a reactionary (or a Red), it is useless for him to protest that he does not hold the basic philosophy that goes with the name. He will simply be told that he is certainly no progressive (or true American) and that he therefore must be the worst type of reactionary (or Red), namely, one who pretends to be progressive (or true American) in order to sabotage progress (or true Americanism). The grounds for denying his protest may seem to be concrete ones — for instance that he fails to support abortion on demand (or fails to oppose a national health system) — but in fact they are merely shibboleths used to force him into a stereotype. And so the individual disappears behind an abstract image.

In the imagination of those who live by stock responses there are no real individuals. Mankind consists of types: the Good Guys and the Bad Guys, the obviously saved and the obviously damned. And these two generalized types can be infallibly distinguished by a simple test. Just as the Good Guys wear white hats and the Bad Guys black ones, so the obviously saved use the "relevant" clichés, slogans, and catchwords, and the obviously damned either repudiate these or else prevaricate and thus prove themselves to be hypocrites.[8]

---

[7]See above, pp. 49-51.

[8]One writer recently asserted that those who deny the fact of the death of God in our age are "not being helpful." The phrase "not being helpful" resembles very closely the blackmailer's response to his victim when the latter is reluctant to pay up promptly, or even the remark of a torturer when his victim withholds the required "confession."

Today "the public," Kierkegaard's "gruesome abstraction," is less often mentioned than it used to be. It has been largely superseded by an even more abstract entity: "modern man" — or, more often — "contemporary man." "The public," after all, might be considered to be a convenient way of speaking about a group of actual people; for we speak of various publics, such as "the reading public," "the discriminating public," and "Liberace's public." But the entity called modern man is as uncontaminated by any hint of particularity as a Platonic idea. Nevertheless, just as the public is a construct of the generalizing imagination, so is modern man. Those claiming to speak for this abstract entity do so because they have discovered it (they affirm) within themselves, and they are anxious to share their discovery with their less fortunate brethren, who remain blind to its presence. Quite astonishing is the conflict of reports about what modern man is like, what he believes, and, especially, what he can no longer believe because he is so completely modern. The variety is only equaled by the certainty with which each discoverer produces his own version — or his latest version, for there is no end to the possibilities of fresh discovery. "One wonders where the left wing existentialist theologians have found their 'modern man,'" wrote Paul van Buren in 1963. "A man who shares the empirical spirit of our age cannot. . . ."[9] But van Buren since has had second thoughts about whether the empirical spirit of our age is entirely determinative of modern man.

The notion that the spirit of our age can be identified with certainty forgets that the spirit of any age is at best a generalization open to dispute. If it is a generalization based on an estimate of the most dominant images used within some particular period of past history, at least there is some concrete evidence to appeal to. But when the period is our own, we have no clear means of sorting out diversity of spirit to be found around us.[10] Ten years ago no one could have guessed the male hair-styles that are general today,

[9] *The Secular Meaning of the Gospel Based on an Analysis of its Language* (New York: Macmillan, 1963), p. 68.

[10] See above, pp. 47-48.

far less what styles of political, philosophical, or religious thought would be around. So to pronounce solemnly about what a man who shares the spirit of our age can or cannot accept is more than slightly ridiculous. It should be obvious that there is no one reality corresponding to the abstraction "modern man."

Perhaps because so many claims to have identified modern man proved so soon to be completely mistaken, the term "contemporary man" has been preferred recently. This term allows us to change our image of modern man more frequently. When we speak of contemporary man we definitely cut out the dead, for they are no longer our contemporaries. But we also suggest that even the modern men who we ourselves were a short time ago no longer represent contemporary man, whose spirit we now share. Of course, it does become difficult to make any statement at all about the nature of contemporary man, since he may change completely before we have finished setting down the first sentence of our account of him.

A consistently thought-out concept, however, is the last thing that a catchword is likely to inspire, and few of those speaking about contemporary man worry about how he is to be identified — other current catchwords take care of that. The point is that families of catchwords are developed because the images underlying each of them are congenial. Thus there can be little doubt that the chief attraction of the catchword "contemporary man" is that, even more than "modern man," it makes so suitable a companion for "relevance." How can anything truly contemporary fail to be also truly relevant, when relevance is connected with "keeping pace"? Stated in terms of our automobile image, the contemporary model must be the relevant one. Anything already on the scrap heap cannot be relevant, and many models still running (modern) may be outdated and their scrapping more than overdue.[11]

[11]The automobile image conforms to the pattern of thinking in abstract entities. Individual cars are identified simply as one of a class ("the 1968 Olds"), each possessing the virtues and defects of that class. The slogan, "Buy a '73 car now," suggests that being a contemporary model is even

Relevance and Idolatry

Reference has been made in this chapter to the "cult" of relevance. But apart from taking one or two examples of the use of this and related catchwords from present-day religious writers, the cult has not been connected with any specifically religious consciousness or the links shown between uncritical enthusiasm for relevance and the practice of idolatry.

Nevertheless, the current preoccupation with the supposedly urgent need for relevance and for concentrating on the supposedly unique requirements of contemporary man is a preoccupation that seems to have infiltrated the ranks of the theologians. It appears conspicuously in many theologies commended to us as peculiarly adapted to the climate of our age. And here the outlines of modern idolatry become visible. Several of the attitudes of mind pointed out in Part One as characteristic of the idolatrous imagination have appeared again in the analysis of catchwords: a claim to possess sure knowledge, a disdain for unenlightened beliefs, a fascination with abstract powers, and so on. But we have yet to note the significance of those for "the religious situation."

In the mechanism of the stock reaction, however, we can already glimpse the relationship between the cult of relevance and idolatry. In this manifestation of "the imagination of men's hearts" there is to be seen at least a latent repudiation of the worship of the living God and a turning away to seek the protection of other powers believed to be in control of human destiny. Where a desire for relevance takes the place of a desire for truth, relevance has been elevated into an absolute power — or at any rate an important manifestation of that power. Where sharing in the spirit of our age is allowed to become so important that it dictates what belief we can or cannot hold, the spirit of the age ("the god of this world") has been elevated into the source

more important than being a particular type of model. The greater abstraction takes precedence over the lesser, which is more concrete and therefore less relevant!

of revelation, the bearer of the word of truth . . . or of relevance, since relevance has replaced truth.

Biblical witness declares that the Spirit of truth issues from the Father and guides into all truth those who confess the name of Jesus Christ (John 15:26; 16:13). Believers in the stock response, on the other hand, replace the authority of the Bible by the authority of clichés, slogans, and catch-words. They await, instead of the Spirit of truth, the spirit of relevance, which will lead them into entire and perfect relevance. They confess the name of a "gruesome abstrac-tion," contemporary man, as the one who is the bearer of the spirit of relevance. As Jesus said of the Spirit, "he will take what is mine and declare it unto you" (John 16:14 RSV), so these latter-day believers expect that the spirit of relevance will make known to them what is essentially belonging to contemporary man. And the father of contem-porary man? It is impossible, of course, that this abstract entity called contemporary man can come from human parents. All human parents that might have been responsible for bringing him into the world are noncontemporary, people of another "nature" altogether. They belong to the old order that has not "kept pace" and has come to be replaced by contemporary man with the new order guided by the spirit of relevance.

The god from whom contemporary man has come and from whom the spirit of relevance issues is the subject of the next chapter.

5

THE GREAT GOD CHANGE

Upward Still and Onward

Since the seventeenth century, when man began to picture the world in terms of the machines he made, the image of technological change has been potent. Because technology is progressive, changing constantly as increasing knowledge of the physical world makes possible the development of new techniques for subduing and controlling it to serve the needs of mankind, it is imagined that the continually improved machine is an adequate analogy for the whole of experienced reality. In order to permit unending improvements in the technological field there must be no power residing in the nature of things to cry "Halt!" Progress must be the eternal law underlying the universe. Moreover, the religious faith by means of which successive generations have sustained themselves cannot be an exception to this law. Faith, too, must be continually revised and move forward with the times, producing for men's changing needs ever improved "models."

The words of James Russell Lowell are well known and have been sung enthusiastically by Christian congregations for a century:

> New occasions teach new duties;
>   Time makes ancient good uncouth;
> They must upward still and onward
>   Who would keep abreast of truth.

Yet perhaps Lowell, a good Victorian living in the heyday of confidence in scientific advancement and the betterment of the human race through each new conquest of nature, could be more readily persuaded of the inevitability of progress than we are likely to be today. Living as we do in the age of the intercontinental ballistic missile and napalm, of brainwashing and skyjacking, of rising crime rates and urban violence, we may pause to wonder whether modern good is actually so couth as it is supposed to be. One suspects that if Lowell himself were called back into the turmoil of the last third of the twentieth century, he would be thoroughly appalled by what would seem to him to be the barbarity of our present manners and morals. Certainly, he would judge the vocabulary of speakers at a Women's Liberation rally of the 1970s most uncouth in comparison with that used by ladies of the 1870s. "Upward still and onward" sounds splendid. But, after our machines have carried us up and on the mountain-slope of history, is there anything awaiting us at the summit except the Doomsday Machine?

In point of fact, the fears of today are by no means new. At the very beginning of the Industrial Revolution, which was to bring about the wide popular conviction of the inevitability of progress, Mary Shelley wrote her novel *Frankenstein*. In this story Frankenstein, the archetype of the scientist-technologist, rashly created the monster who was to destroy him. Stories of machines taking over the world have been common ever since, but this particular story has made an indelible impression such as no other has been able to do. *Frankenstein* so vividly portrays the gulf between the intention of technologists to benefit humanity and the actual results, which, however beneficial, always have unforeseen side-effects that may well prove catastrophic. In the inhuman monster of Frankenstein's creation, the abstract nature of the machine world is given a memorable image. The whole story reminds us that belief in inevitable progress is essentially a dream. Anyone who deliberately embraces a dream because it is more pleasant than reality is insecure, for he knows what he is unwilling to admit — that his dream may turn suddenly into a nightmare. By bringing this insecurity out of the unconsciousness into which it has been thrust, and by giving the nightmare a fictional form, *Frankenstein* reassures the believer in progress through technology and allows him to continue in his dream. He thinks, "How horrible! But, after all, it's only a made-up story. Absurd things like that can't actually happen." Thus the momentary vision of terror actually increases the pleasure of the dream.

The notion that the machine was a completely adequate picture of the world, all the same, had threatening implications for the vision of man's place in the universe. In the eighteenth century and, more particularly, the nineteenth, enthusiasm for scientific and technological progress allowed many to feel quite satisfied with a purely mechanistic view. Others demanded a philosophy of life that would prove beyond doubt that man, the machine-maker, was not himself a machine and so would always be able to control his handiwork. The religious view that there lay within man a living "spirit," operating beyond the sphere of his body and so beyond biological laws that could be explained as mechanisms, was all-important for the belief that man was "different."

The philosophy of Descartes broke with the past and today is still reckoned the first *modern* philosophy. By accepting the scientific world-view, Descartes set philosophy on a new track; and his views largely determined the course philosophy was to take in the succeeding centuries. Descartes took over from traditional Christianity the understanding of man as a spiritual being needing to know himself created by an omnipotent deity. But his presentation of the human spirit as (in Gilbert Ryle's phrase) "the ghost in the machine" was seen as an unstable amalgam of the traditional and the modern. A consistently modern estimate of man was demanded, one that found the human spirit a place not requiring traditional notions of "the supernatural" God of traditional Christianity to be imported. Since the modern world-view assumed the law of progress, spirit in man had to be progressive also. And deity, too, had to conform to the idea of progress (supposing that an idea of God as pure or ultimate spirit should be found necessary to provide the ground for the human spirit).

Immanuel Kant found a solution in the idea of God as disclosed within man's innate capacity for self-legislation. In his tract *What is Enlightenment?*, he shows us the background against which his understanding of man and God were worked out. His thesis is that the age is not an "enlightened age" but an "age of enlightenment." That is, it is going upward and onward. And he looks forward to progress chiefly as the dead hand of authority is removed in matters of religion. Once men are allowed to choose what to believe out of themselves, enlightenment will take a giant stride forward. The inference is that what distinguishes man from a machine is the spirit within him. Before this spirit is liberated and expresses only what arises spontaneously from itself, man is governed by mechanical laws such as prevail throughout the whole universe except the human spirit.

Kant's name for the human spirit was "the practical reason." He limited practical reason to the sphere of moral understanding, but deduced from its operation the reality of freedom, immortality, and God — in other words, what are usually referred to as "spiritual truths."[1] Hegel sought to overcome Kant's restriction of the human spirit to the merely ethical dimension of experience. He did so by bringing not only the visible universe but the whole of reality within the law of inevitable progress. Like Descartes's, Kant's vision of the world made a division between the physical world operating by mechanical laws and the interior world of spirit reached through man's unique self-consciousness. Hegel tore down this long-continuing barrier by making all reality consist of spirit. There is no independent material realm of mechanical order over against which the human spirit must assert

[1] Kant distinguished "the laws of nature," which are the concern of physics, from "the laws of freedom," which are the concern of ethics.

itself. If we seek to know matter as such, we find it only "as that in which consciousness weaves and moves inarticulately within itself."[2] All is comprehended within God as the infinite spirit that comes to consciousness in man as finite spirit. Furthermore, continuing development according to its own inherent laws is the very essence of the spiritual substance that is God. The history of the universe is the history of spirit developing into self-consciousness in man and proceeding towards perfect self-knowledge through mankind's spiritual development. Hegel ends his *Phenomenology of Mind* with these lines adapted from Schiller:

> *The chalice of this realm of spirits*
> *Foams forth to God His own Infinitude.*[3]

For Hegel "upward still and onward" is not simply an idea conceived by man's imagination. It is the very law of the universe — and man is both the bearer and the executor of this law.

The Vegetable Image

Hegel's philosophy appeared to be the culmination of the "modern" vision of the world. At one stroke it established the modern belief in inevitable progress and guaranteed the reality of the human spirit. It broke free from the authority of traditional Christianity, with its "unbelievable" concept of an objective personal God ruling over the world like a king upon a throne; and at the same time it freed man from the fear that he was no more than a cog in the world-machine. By showing the unity of the human spirit with the Divine Spirit, while keeping the former dependent upon the latter, it had saved religion without denying science. Christianity, indeed, could

---

[2] *The Phenomenology of Mind*, translated by J. B. Baillie (London: Allen & Unwin, 1910), p. 592.

[3] *Ibid.*, p. 808.

be retained — once it had been interpreted in terms of this all-embracing vision.

Yet no conceptual system, however grandiose, can seem convincing unless the image on which it is founded is acceptable to men's imaginations at the time. By the example that he chose in order to demonstrate how infinite spirit can change and grow without ceasing to be itself, Hegel shows us the basic image on which his system was raised — the image of an organism.

Hegel actually took his illustration from plant life. Already in the previous century David Hume in his *Dialogues Concerning Natural Religion* had pointed out that defenders of the idea of a divine creator of the world had used the image of human workmanship to prove that the existence of the world implied a supreme maker. But, Hume said, it could be argued that the world resembles more nearly an animal or a vegetable than it does a watch or a knitting loom, "the machines of human invention." It is possible that Hegel may have known of Hume's comparison, but he almost certainly took his inspiration from another source.

Hegel himself and German idealistic philosophy in general were strongly influenced by the Romantic literary movement, a movement that had turned away from the mechanistic civilization being raised around them by science and its works. The Romantic writers went to "unspoiled nature," particularly to woods and flowers, to find an image of the human spirit. In the man-made world, they believed, man's spirit was denied growth and became as dead and mechanical and inhuman as a machine. In living nature, his spirit discovered kinship with another and a vital world. It was likely enough, then, that Hegel should base his own picture of the universe on the analogy of a small seed growing into a complex and beautiful plant. Just as a seed carries its pattern of growth complete but undeveloped within itself, so does pure spirit before the world process is set in motion. As a seed grows into a plant by being set in an element unlike itself (the "dead" mineral element of earth), so spirit transforms itself into world by trusting itself to its opposite, matter. And, as the power of growth of a plant is communicated through its separate cells — each one brought into being by the plant, yet each one truly participating in the life of the plant and making it what it was not before — so man the finite spirit, by participating in the life of infinite spirit, also makes God what he was not before.

Organic nature, nevertheless, does not simply go ceaselessly upward and onward. It goes in cycles. Everything in nature, as Aristotle observed long ago, is in the process of coming to be and passing away; and the latter process is set in motion just as soon as the former begins. Hegel's decision to consider only the coming to be proves that the "modern" vision (as distinct from the traditional view, both Christian and Greek) determined his outlook. He held, as a matter of course, to the belief in inevitable progress; and belief in automatic progress goes, not with the image of natural growth, but with the image of constantly improving machines. In this he showed himself to be a true son of the Enlightenment. For the men of the Enlightenment chose the image of constantly increasing light, forgetting apparently that in this world the light-giving sun that rises must also set.[4]

The tension between these two distinct and irreconcilable images — the organic and the mechanistic — was to dissolve Hegelianism as a unitary movement. Alfred North Whitehead once remarked that philosophies are not

---

[4]Man-made artificial light, of course, is not under this necessity. But then the result of living by this kind of light is to *extinguish* the light of the human spirit. A telling illustration of this truth is found in George Orwell's *1984*. The hero, Winston Smith, meets a man whom he believes to be a kindred spirit in rebellion against the inhuman, mechanistic regime under which all men live in 1984. Smith writes of this man in his diary: "We shall meet in a place where there is no darkness." But his dream of progress to a future of enlightened freedom turns to a nightmare when he discovers his imagined ally to be the head of the Mind-Control Police. The two men do indeed meet in a place where there is no darkness, but it is the torture chamber of the ironically named Ministry of Love where perpetually burning electric light wipes out the distinction between night and day. This image stands for the ultimate inhumanity, which denies the natural rhythms of life, lacking which the human spirit is robbed of all sense of personal existence.

proved wrong, but instead go out of fashion. Later they are rediscovered, trimmed up a little, and brought back as a new discovery. Whitehead's observation is quite understandable if our thesis about the primacy of the imagination over thinking is accepted. Since the appeal of every world-view rests on the images prompting it, not on its conceptual cogency, a change in the focus of men's imagination and thus of their interests can spell the sudden death of the most widely acclaimed philosophical system. So it was with Hegelian philosophy. It split — almost at once — into two schools, each following one of the two images that he had tried to bring together. The right-wing Hegelians, who included most of those thinkers with a predominantly religious concern, held to the organic image. They stressed the active participation of the human spirit in the infinite spirit. The left-wing Hegelians stressed the inevitability of progress operating through the iron laws governing technical development. Their demand was for man's social and political betterment without delay, so they abandoned Hegel's pan-spiritism for materialism.

Karl Marx, the most famous Hegelian of the left, was faithful to the image of the world as an artifact. So he tied the course of developing humanity to the development of new means of production. Man was the maker who through making made himself. Nevertheless, after Hegel, the organic image was never totally effaced. This can be seen in the fact that orthodox Marxism insists on *dialectical* materialism, considering mechanistic materialism a heresy as deadly as the opposite heresy of spiritualism. Marx's replacement for Hegel's absolute spirit is the material life-process. It is a curious hybrid, when looked on as an image, for it suggests either a self-conscious and self-developing machine or else a natural organism that grows by controlling its environment instead of being dependent on it. A tool-using vegetable is a very odd monster indeed!

Hegelians of the right often developed the organic image to a remarkable extent. For example, Ralph Waldo

Emerson's famous Harvard Divinity School Address of 1838 began with a prose-poem about summer, the season of vegetable life. "The grass grows," rhapsodizes Emerson, "the buds burst, the meadow is spotted with fire and gold in the tint of flowers."[5] That this is no rhetorical flourish but an integral part of Emerson's presentation of his religious standpoint soon appears. For he moves on to argue that the healthy face of nature is made diseased by the attempt of "historical Christianity" to speak to man about God in "a traditionary and limited way," instead of appealing to man to recognize God present in himself. Jesus was the true prophet, announcing the incarnation of deity in everyman. And only when everyman perceives this truth in himself — that he is an infinite soul — will the day arise when faith will "blend with the light of rising and of setting suns, with the flying cloud, the singing bird, and the breath of flowers."[6]

Emerson's address does not develop a cumulative argument, but circles around its central theme. If we look for it, though, we can see how this theme continues the image of his opening words about the grass and the flowers, picturing the growth of the spirit of humanity in terms of natural growth. Emerson suggests that, as in the visible world of nature, healthy growth in the inner world is marked by the constant production of new growth. That the Christian church is stationary is, for Emerson, proof of its diseased state. The flowering of the spirit is marked by new love, new faith, new sight, new hope, new revelation, and a coming new teacher (the perfect flower of spirituality?) who "shall see the world to be the mirror of the soul." Reliance on anything exterior to the life-springs of spiritual consciousness or old and set in form (such as Bible and creeds) has the coldness of death on it. The institutional church is cold. Science is cold. Legislated morality is cold.

[5]"The Divinity School Address" in *Three Prophets of Religious Liberalism: Channing — Emerson — Parker* (Boston: Beacon Press, 1961), p. 90.
[6]*Ibid.*, p. 102.

Thus Emerson states his case in terms of the vegetable image. According to this image, the spirit of humanity is always in danger of being killed by the frosts of set forms or deformed by efforts to bend it in ways contrary to its natural growth. But it is most in danger of not drawing from within itself the power of luxuriant growth given by its organic nature. The flower of spirituality will not bloom only if the spiritual plant fails to behave as a plant should do.

The Perennial New

With the rise of the two wings of Hegelianism we are already in the phase of the "modern" world that shows most of the features of the "contemporary" world. By this time, many of the pivotal catchwords currently in use are established. And since then we have been living under the shadow of the two Hegelian images: the mechanistic and the organic. The mechanistic image has predominated, as is not surprising in view of the tremendous transformation of the external world by technology during the past century-and-a-half. But the organic image is there also, though often submerged. And at the present moment we are seeing its rebirth.[7] This has been repeated at intervals whenever urbanized men have begun to feel acutely that they have lost contact with living nature and its vital powers of growth. Then the technological dream of upward and onward seems to have turned into a nightmare in which a man-made tower of steel and concrete, supposed to raise us to the heaven of our desires, has turned into an imprisoning cage against which the wings of the human spirit beat in vain.

Yet the Hegelian organic image is not content to stay within the limits of the natural world. It, too, looks to an ascent to heaven achieved by the human spirit; and it turns against technological progress only when the quest

[7]See below, pp. 112, 117-21.

THE GREAT GOD CHANGE

for Utopia in the external world is frustrated. Then it follows the internal route, along which the infinite desires of the human spirit seem to offer an escape from man's finite existence and its accompanying frustrations. Either way, what we are having recommended to us is a faith in salvation from history. We are being invited to run away from the exacting, unsatisfactory world of historical existence and to embrace an abstract, ideological world in which everything flows effortlessly into the shape of our desires.

We hear over and over complaints that traditional Christianity has not kept pace, or that it is unbelievable to contemporary man. Such complaints actually have nothing to do with the events going on in our times or with the situation of real people living in our particular period of history. They have to do with an attitude of mind — a quality of the imagination — that has been around for a long time. It is an attitude of despising historical continuity — as typified in tradition — and trying to ignore it. So we have the paradox that the doctrine which exalts the contemporary is itself a doctrine that changes hardly at all over the years. Were the language only a little updated, there would be nothing to tell us that the following extract from Emerson's "Divinity School Address" was written not this year but nearly a hundred and forty years ago.

> And now, my brothers, you will ask, What in these desponding days can be done by us? The remedy is already declared in the ground of our complaint of the Church. We have contrasted the Church with the Soul. In the soul, then, let the redemption be sought. Wherever a man comes, there comes revolution. The old is for slaves. When a man comes, all books are legible, all things transparent, all religions are forms . . . [The falsehood of the Church's theology is that] true Christianity, — a faith like Christ's in the infinitude of man, — is lost. None believeth in the soul of man, but only in some man or person old and departed . . . Once leave your own knowledge of God, your own sentiment, and take secondary knowledge, as St. Paul's, or George Fox's, or Swedenborg's, and you get wide with God with every year this secondary form lasts, and if, as

now, for centuries, — the chasm yawns in breadth, that men can scarcely be convinced there is in them anything divine.[8]

Present-day guidebooks to the New Christianity, the New Theology, Relevant Faith for Contemporary Man, Radical Freedom, Faith for the Twenty-First Century, and the like are full of this type of heady generalization ringing the changes on "out with the old and restricting, in with the new and liberating." The point is that here "old" and "new" have nothing to do with time and men's concrete existence in history. They are abstract terms, constructs of the imagination elevated to the position of powers ruling over the human spirit.

Thus, when we are urged to adopt "a truly contemporary faith," we are not being asked to accept a faith previously unknown and just recently discovered. We are being pressured into accepting a myth. According to this myth, the whole universe is enslaved by a wicked tyrant called The Old, whose power is being challenged continually by a young hero called The New. In every age these two powers contend. When we understand that this is the truth about the human situation, we will recognize that any faith that does not admit the myth is under the power of The Old, and any faith that does teach it is on the side of The New. If we reject the myth, we are slaves. If we accept it, we join in the present warfare on the side of the liberating power of The New.

Similarly, when we are told that the traditional institutional church is outdated, we are not being informed about specific aspects of the shortcomings of the Christian church. We are being indoctrinated with the dogma that all religions are forms of the immediate intuition in the human spirit of its own divinity. It follows that any church teaching an historical revelation is betraying "true Christianity." It does not matter, therefore, that a particular belief may be historically old and preached for a century or longer. If it is a belief professing faith in The New it

[8]*Three Prophets of Religious Liberalism*, pp. 107-08.

is new, since The New is our present consciousness of the infinitude of the human spirit.

Martin Buber once wrote: "It is a modern superstition that the character of an age acts as fate for the next. One lets it prescribe what is possible to do and hence what is permitted. One surely cannot swim against the stream, one says."[9] The superstition indicated by Buber comes from despising historical existence. In historical existence people actually live and, though influenced by "the spirit of the age," are not tied to it. But belief in inevitable and irreversible progress (the mechanistic image) or in an infinite human spirit passing through different forms but living only in its present form of consciousness (the organic image) isolates man in The New and makes his own past inaccessible to him. The past is literally the *dead* past and lays its dead hand on him, thus appearing, as Buber says, as if it were a fate. What has gone by can have no meaning for him. The consequence is that he is locked in the present moment as in a prison.

Consider, for example, the following statement by Thomas J. J. Altizer:

> It is my conviction that the contemporary theologian is most dangerous when he attempts to maintain that the ancient and traditional form of faith can be spoken in our situation or, for that matter, that it even has a latent or potential meaning which can bring life to our world. Nothing delights the enemy of faith so much as the idea that faith is ever the same, yesterday, today, and forever, with the obvious corollary that faith is hopelessly archaic and irrelevant today. The theologian enhances the charge of irrelevance when he identifies faith with its ancient form or even presumes that we can know an ancient faith in a living form. Moreover, I am persuaded that, at whatever point we employ a traditional theological form or language, we are therein engaged in the process of annulling the contemporary reality of faith, thereby not simply diluting but also assaulting a faith which can and does speak in our time.[10]

[9]"God and the Spirit of Man," *Eclipse of God* (New York: Harper, 1957), p. 129.

[10]"Commentary" (on Michael Novak's "The New Relativism in American Theology") in *The Religious Situation: 1968,* edited by Donald R. Cutler (Boston: Beacon, 1968), pp. 242-43.

The astonishing thing about Altizer's statement is that he seems so anxiously protective about "the contemporary reality of faith" and so supine before the sneers of this abstract figure, "the enemy of faith," with his charges of irrelevance. If a faith can and does speak in our time, why not let it make its own way through its own persuasiveness? Why speak as though it were a tiny, frail flower liable any minute to be trodden down by assaults from the presuming boots of dangerous theologians? And why should Altizer not simply tell that terrible enemy, if he ever meets him, to grow up and not confuse bandying around silly catchwords with adult discussion about serious topics?

Furthermore, Altizer himself used traditional language — including such ancient words and phrases as "therein," "thereby," and "ever the same." Evidently, he expects to be understood when he uses this very traditional language in order to tell us that the traditional language of faith has no living meaning today. This seems rather inconsistent.

Actually, of course, Altizer is quite consistent within his own dogmatic framework, which is one that idolizes the abstract idea of The New. His dogma assumes that we cannot know ancient faith in a living form, because, no matter how many people actually live by some ancient faith at the present moment, their faith has been declared *a priori* to be "not living." Equally, Altizer can readily find meaning in some bygone faith (the faith of Hegel, for example) and preach it today. But by definition this ancient faith is not ancient but modern and a contemporary reality. It is an expression of what might be called the Perennial New.

Altizer's defensiveness is quite clearly a reaction to protect a specific faith, namely, faith in the myth of the Perennial New. This is the faith of those who believe that they have been saved out of historical existence to live in a pure dimension of abstract "historicity" manifesting itself in contemporary "moments." Historicity is quite different from the ordinary history known to actual individuals in day-to-day life. Historicity is the nonhistorical dimension in which we discover the Perennial New bequeathed to us by the spirit of the previous age and now carried in the spirit of the contemporary age.

In the eyes of all those who believe in the myth of the Perennial New, anyone who presumes to suggest that we are not tied by our fate and compelled to find meaning only in the contemporary form of faith is, of course, a threat and a walking blasphemy. Such a person has the effrontery to believe that he is free to move beyond the prison walls of the contemporary moment and to understand — even to appropriate for himself — forms of faith from the past. Such a person does not ritualistically intone current catchwords, believing them to be revelations to the contemporary mind. He does not vilify the old and automatically sing Hallelujahs in praise of the new; and he will not be intimidated by being told that he is on that account a dangerous reactionary, secretly deifying the old and cherishing a vicious hatred for all that is new. He can appreciate the old and the new; but, as an individual living in history where "old" and "new" are relative and interdependent terms, he is tired of hearing endlessly repeated old myths about the Perennial New.

Change, the Immutable King

The god from whom the spirit of this age issues, the god who sends contemporary man into the world so that the spirit of the age may testify of the things that belong to him, the god who gives the Perennial New to those who show forth the fruits of relevance, the god who guarantees inevitable progress — the name of this god is Change, for he is the guarantor of continual change as an Absolute. So long as he rules in his nonhistorical heaven, the law that everything changes, upward and onward, can never change. In him the Perennial New is ever new and powerful and the Perennial Old is continually being cast down into the hell of irrelevance.

That the cult of relevance and faith in the Perennial New are actual exercises in present-day idolatry first occurred to me when I read a short book by a Catholic layman, Christopher Derrick's *Trimming the Ark: Catholic Attitudes and the Cult of Change*.[11] Derrick notes how widespread was the reaction of defensive surprise and alarm — such as we noted in the quotation from Altizer — to any suggestion that one need not follow the movement of the time, or (as Buber says) swim with the stream. Derrick writes: "You are not merely a harmless fool, a quixotic dreamer: you have desecrated the shrine and blasphemed the god, provoking the special kind of indignation that is appropriate in such cases." And he continues:

> It is as though change itself had been promoted in men's minds, raised above the role of an excellent creature and given the status of a deity. At one philosophical level this tendency has borne fruit in the recurring attempts to derive a strictly scientific and evolutionary morality, a set of imperatives wholly based upon well established indicatives, inevitably involving in practice something like a deification of the evolutionary process. But the corresponding *mood* is cherished far too widely and too passionately to be regarded as a rational acceptance of demonstrated truth. Twentieth-century man is, for whatever reason, romantically in love with the idea of change itself and for its own sake; the philosophers follow behind, rationalizing that passion as best they can.[12]

Derrick describes the emergence, within the cult of change, of what he calls Obsessive Contemporaneity focused on the Mythological Now. The latter is what we have been referring to as the myth of the Perennial New. I have chosen this name because it is important to notice not merely the present form taken by what Derrick rightly terms "a dramatic hypostatization of the present moment, the Now," but its historical pedigree. The love of change we observe around us today is more than a quirk in the temper of twentieth-century man. It is the acceptance by

[11]New York: P. J. Kenedy & Sons, 1968.
[12]*Trimming the Ark*, pp. 23, 25.

many people of a particular vision of life. Although this vision and the myth justifying it have been around for a long time, it is urged on us as *the* form of faith for our present age, something absolutely contemporary, relevant, and new. As Derrick observes, for anything to be accepted as participating in the Mythological Now, it must have been widely publicized. For this reason, I have shown the great part played by slogans and catchwords in obtaining the mood appropriate to the worship of the Great God Change. The stock response, and not discriminating thought, is the oblation this god demands.

Idolatry is turning away from the living God to worship "strange gods." In Part One it was noted how already in New Testament times the image of abstract monotheism, born of sophisticated contempt of local deities, was beginning to supplant graven images in men's imagination. The gods men turned to worship were increasingly abstract powers conceived to be in absolute control of human destiny.

The Great God Change seems to be the controlling power most favored today. And if people do not build temples and offer sacrifices to him it is because such activities would not be appropriate to the kind of god he is. His impersonality is the first article in the unwritten creed confessing his godhead, and his true believers' contempt for any kind of anthropomorphic language in religion is absolute. Indeed, this contempt is the chief weapon the worshipers of the Great God Change use against traditional Christianity. The notion of a God "out there," a God who can be pictured as an old man with a white beard, is dismissed as utterly unbelievable and far below the momentary consideration of twentieth-century man. Any attempt on the part of Christians to suggest that these crude images do not accurately represent the God whom they confess is simply put aside as evasion tactics.

The Great God Change, all the same, is invested with the supreme power which is understood in the Judeo-Christian tradition to belong to the living God. For instance, he is often invoked as the giver of life. Change, we are told (often from Christian preachers in the pulpits of Christian churches), is life. So we must flee from what is old and static and welcome everything that is new and dynamic. We are assured, too, by many theologians that God can no longer be imagined by means of a static model. He must be constant, creative change. (It is true that these theologians also speak of bipolar theism. But this is because the Great God Change in order to be a god must be immutable in part of his essence, in order to remain the ground of all change and in order to guarantee that all change shall be unidirectional — upward still and onward.) We are exhorted on all sides, therefore, to welcome change, to work for change, to initiate social change, and to follow those who are the agents of change.

Until recently, change was chiefly thought to come through evolution. Hegel's evolutionary theory of world history had been substantiated in the biological field by Darwin. So, as we had evolved from the primeval slime, we were destined in the fulness of time to ascend to god-like perfection. Master of his own fate, man must take on the responsibility of being "the steersman of the cosmos" — and then we would know the name of the true God.[13]

Such a view — expounded by Pierre Teilhard de Chardin, for example, as the true meaning of Christianity as seen by the contemporary spirit (a claim made previously by Hegel) — is still quite widely accepted. But now many worshipers of the Great God Change have come to the conclusion that slow evolutionary change is not a sufficient offering to lay on the altar. "Radical" and "revolutionary" are the most popular words used to describe the oblations thought to be most pleasing to his godhead, since this god helps those who help themselves. We cannot change too far or too fast if we are to avoid being thought lukewarm in his service.

Revolution was central to the thinking of most of the

[13]"Man, seen as the steersman of the cosmos, is the only starting point we have for a viable doctrine of God." Harvey Cox's Afterword in *The Secular City Debate,* edited by Daniel Callahan (New York: Macmillan, 1966), p. 199.

Hegelians of the left; and Emerson's dictum "Wherever a man comes, there comes revolution" reminds us that Hegelians of the right also stressed the idea, though not in a political sense. The most influential cultural prophets in recent years have been almost unanimous in support of some variety of *radical revolution*. (I am thinking here of names such as Marshall McLuhan, Herbert Marcuse, and Norman O. Brown.) Regardless of the individual programs each advances, each agrees that only drastic change — revolutionary change — can reflect the spirit of the age and usher in Utopia. And they ask us to believe that Utopia will assuredly come — or that it has already come in principle — if only we know how to welcome it by radically altering ourselves to be worthy of it.

Similarly, best-sellers like Charles A. Reich's *The Greening of America* and Alvin Toffler's *Future Shock* promise that the best of all possible Brave New Worlds is just around the corner. The only condition of its appearance is our willingness to recognize the changes that are upon us and to adapt ourselves so that we become channels through which the Great God Change can express himself. Reich thinks that a new type of consciousness has spontaneously evolved in our age: Consciousness III. If we give ourselves over to this mysterious power, it will free us from all our hang-ups. "Whatever it touches it beautifies," says Reich, "and every barrier falls before it."[14] At least Toffler admits that the pace of change around us can be killing. Yet he suggests that if we take this poison in small doses, we can immunize ourselves from its deadly effects, absorb it safely, and be far heathier and happier than ever before. In any case, he is sure that change cannot be halted or reversed. We must go along with it wherever it takes us . . . forever, it seems.

The Abstract Gifts of an Abstract God

We began our examination of the nature of idolatry as

[14]*The Greening of America* (New York: Random House, 1970), p. 395.

the Bible tells us of it by speaking about the dynamics of the nonexistent.[15] Change is one of the good gifts given to us by the good Creator. Given the status of a god, change still continues to serve the Creator's purposes and to bring joy into our lives, but "the imagination of men's hearts" has perverted our understanding of the power of change. As a deity the Great God Change does not exist; nevertheless, when it is imagined to exist, it exercises a real power over our lives that has real consequences.

The living God alone gives gifts that are concretely beneficial, reflecting his grace, his righteousness, and his mercy. Other powers made into gods have no personal attributes. The only gifts they can give are abstract ones. In Greek mythology, when mortals asked the gods for gifts — whether immortality or the power to turn things to gold or prophecy — those gifts brought ruin to those who received them. It is the same with the gifts that we beg from the gods we ourselves have made. For the Creator did not make us abstractly. He made us for this very concretely individual world. And if we serve one power within it and expect it to serve us, we try to make the world into something that it cannot be and will resemble the less the harder we try to transform it to our chosen blueprint. To look for good gifts from the creature instead of from the Creator is to cherish dreams that must in the end turn into nightmares.

Manifestly, change is not synonymous with life. It is no more than one element in life. Truly essential to life is continuity, which is change with sameness. Life must conserve as well as transform; and change without continuity is wholly destructive. Yet, wherever the Great God Change is invoked, radical change is given as the answer to all our problems and promised as the key to the abundant life.

Radical change, indeed, can be quite easily achieved. Consider, for example, anyone who takes a jump out of a tenth-floor window. Looking at the result on the street below, no one can doubt that a complete break has been

[15]See above, pp. 12-16.

made with the status quo. Within the human organism, too, radical change is quite frequent. It goes by the name of cancer. A cancer cell has been described as one that has forgotten how to behave in a body. In the light of that definition we may understand how the blind worship of change encourages cancerous growths in individual, social, and spiritual existence.

Refusal to change, of course, may equally have disastrous effects. But the concrete historical situation alone must guide both the pace and the direction of change. Loss of continuity through uncontrolled change means death. We can never afford to forget this. Indeed, without a reliable memory, by means of which continuity is preserved, we cannot exist for long. In the realm of human behavior and thinking, continuity is guaranteed by tradition. No one makes himself, and no one can make anything of himself without drawing on a tradition that he has inherited. However violently he rebels against received traditions, he will still be influenced by them far more than he realizes. When he seeks to make a complete break with an inherited tradition, he can do so only by drawing on another tradition. As I have pointed out, those who scorn everything traditional and worship change still in fact draw their theory of revolt, their cult of the new, and even the language of their slogans and catchwords out of an existing tradition.

Respect for facts, however, is not what the Great God Change encourages. The biblical description of engaging in idolatry is having "exchanged the truth about God for a lie" (Rom. 1:25 RSV). All monotheistic gods are *jealous* gods, but the living God is jealous for the integrity of his name, because in him are righteousness and truth. He is jealous on account of his people, commanding them to choose the ways of truth and live. The gods of abstract monotheism are gods only because they have been given that status by "the imagination of men's hearts." And so they are jealous only to maintain the stock response that preserves their power. So the Great God Change turns men's hearts away from concrete realities to abstractions that, given substance through slogans and catchwords, are imagined to be the very stuff of reality. Since the god is no Creator, he has no love for the created order and no desire that individuals should live. Worshipers of a god become made in his likeness, and the Great God Change passes on his ruthlessness to his followers.

In the last chapter we saw that the cult of relevance denies dissenters any right to their opinions, which is actually the same as denying them the right to be.[16] The reason for such intolerance should now be clear. The worshiper of the Great God Change asserts that one form of faith alone is contemporary and all other forms are (in Altizer's phrase) "not living." Only those who accept the Perennial New are living. The others may exist, but having failed to respond to the spirit of the age they are as good as dead. They have chosen the slavery of the old. The old laws said that the slave, not recognized as a "person" in the eyes of the law, could not even move to defend his own life, for "the necessity of his condition is upon him." In the eyes of the worshipers of change, the "necessity of the condition" of the old, the noncontemporary, and the traditional is to yield unconditionally to the new, the radical, and the revolutionary. This applies equally to those who represent the forces of reaction. They have no meaningful voice to speak with, anyway. They just exist in history. Those who live in the sense of having the contemporary spirit, on the other hand, have been saved from history. They live in the liberty of the present moment and speak to their time, the time of the truly contemporary world. They have accepted their fate to be contemporary men. Why then should they tolerate "dangerous" individuals who "assault" genuinely contemporary faith by insisting on outmoded forms of faith?

Abstract life, of course, is by no means the same as life understood in relation to concretely existing individuals, that life which the Gospels promise (Matt. 7:14; Luke 12:15; John 10:10). A clear illustration of the dif-

[16]See above, pp. 71-74.

ference is provided by John Pairman Brown, who speaks of "an authentic triple revolution of life: the *green* revolution of conservation, the *peace* revolution of liberated community, the *inner* revolution of integrity." These three, so he affirms, tell us that men and women today are "for the first time daring to become themselves. *The human race has issued a non-negotiable demand for life.*"[17]

The final sentence, italicized by Brown, would have my vote as the most ludicrous sentence in contemporary writing (though I do not doubt that there are equally worthy contenders that have escaped my notice). If anything is certain about this world, it is that life is a gift, one we keep as long as we are wise and resolute and resourceful. Life cannot be made the subject of a demand, far less a nonnegotiable one. That the human race has survived so far shows that men and women have made a certain response to the necessary conditions for maintaining life. If they enter on an "authentic revolution" to demand life, it is quite certain that their chances of survival will be greatly lessened. Their survival will be precarious to the extent that they are encouraged to ignore the traditional wisdom that mankind has inherited, a wisdom learned over the centuries through long and tough struggle with the forces threatening his continued existence. And the changes necessary to survival will not be wisely made if they are made on the basis of inflated expectations of the outcome of a revolution in which *for the first time* men and women have dared to become themselves.

A contemporary journalist who has made a study of archaeology has a pertinent word to say in this connection. Observing that "what archaeology offers is an antidote to hysteria," he goes on to comment:

> There is manifestly a deep need that is satisfied by a knowledge of our collective pedigree; without a past we are psychic orphans. An understanding of our origins may not provide a "guide for action," but it can give us the self-confidence we so desperately need to find a plan for our common survival. For this reason, I

[17] *Planet on Strike* (New York: Seabury, 1970), p. 2; italics in the text.

find grotesque the belief that the message of the past is essentially discouraging. After a century of demolition work on an illusion-ridden past steeped in chauvinism, it is ironic that a new generation of radicals should scorn the past because it might make less credible an illusion-ridden future.[18]

Illusions, however, make up the very fabric of idolatrous faith. The Great God Change, like Baal (I Kings 18:28-29) and the Artemis of Ephesus (Acts 19:28-29), maintains his godhead by promoting hysteria. The childish fancy that "we are the first" can thrive only if we are too ignorant, complacent, and steeped in the shallow generalizations of slogans and catchwords to face concrete realities. Thinking that those who find value in the old — the noncontemporary — are slaves, we rave on about the coming certain liberation into life, which we have unconditionally demanded, until we are sobered up by concrete reality to find that we have sold ourselves into slavery. Then — if we are still around to know anything at all — we discover that abstract gods can give none but abstract gifts. That is the subject of our next chapter.

---

[18]Karl E. Meyer, *The Pleasures of Archeology* (London: Andre Deutsch, 1971), p. 285. Meyer also comments, "The notion that everything is new is itself old, part of the past which is said to be disposable" (p. 284).

6

THE PROMISED LAND OF LIBERATION

The Dream of Absolute Freedom

Just as the living God led Israel out of bondage in Egypt to the promised land of Canaan, so worshipers of the Great God Change trust their god to lead them out of bondage. The Egypt of oppression from which they dream to be delivered is the Perennial Old, "the old" that is for slaves. It goes by many names. Marx named it the status quo, and enthusiasm for the idea of revolution has kept that name around. It is also called the System, the Establishment, "existing structures," the square world, and of course (in the realm of faith) Traditional Christianity. There is also a promised land towards which those who feel they groan under the oppression of the Perennial Old have set their faces. It goes by the name of liberation.

Freedom is probably the only value against which no one today is willing to say a word — or at least to be heard saying it in public. Freedom is what relevance and change are all about. Love is also popular, but love's appeal gives way whenever the extension of freedom is involved. Love is not thought to be sufficient reason for refusing to bomb, shoot, kidnap, or otherwise liquidate those who are believed to stand in the path of a move towards freedom. Liberation is freedom for the new to

replace the old. It is freedom made absolute. Thus liberation is urged at every level for every section of mankind:
for national groups in all lands, for the sexes separately,
for heterosexual and homosexual relationships, for every
conceivable minority group, and for every human spirit
that feels itself oppressed by an Establishment, System,
law, code, custom, obligation, or any constricting or
limiting bond whatever.

The ideal of liberation has even been singled out as
the motive force of the whole universe. Here is the verdict
of Hans Hofmann:

> Life is constantly evolving toward freedom. It cannot stand still;
> it must go on. The question is whether we move with it or
> whether we — and perhaps the whole human race — become
> deadwood which the evolutionary force discards on the scrap
> heap of history.[1]

Hofmann's declaration of faith in evolution towards
freedom assumes that freedom does not serve man, but
man serves freedom. No individual can imagine that he
enjoys enough freedom for his needs, for if he does he
has not been liberated. Such an individual has been crim-
inally deaf to the voice of cosmic freedom telling him that
he must still go on. And, if the human race refuses to
hear and obey this imperious voice, it will be discarded
as an unworthy instrument for achieving freedom's over-
riding purposes.

This power named freedom must be a mighty figure
indeed, so to command the whole universe. And it seems
that he can be none other than the executive right hand
of the Great God Change. Just as the archangel Michael
is God's agent in defeating the powers of evil holding the
world in bondage (Dan. 10:13; Rev. 12:7-9), the power
of evolutionary freedom seems to perform the same function in relation to the Great God Change. James Kavanaugh writes that "God lives and is born in man's efforts
to be fulfilled and free."[2]

---

[1] *Discovering Freedom* (Boston: Beacon, 1969), p. 93.

[2] *The Birth of God* (New York: Trident, 1969), p. 190.

In *A Modern Priest Looks at His Outmoded Church*, Kavanaugh told how he was led to rebel against the "structures" of the Roman Catholic Church because he found the institutional church irrelevant to the needs of contemporary man. It is plain that the cult of relevance, the worship of the Great God Change, and the quest for the promised land of liberation are three aspects of one idolatrous stance. The interconnection between the three appears in this instance. Kavanaugh started with an emphasis on the primacy of relevance; next he changed his allegiance under what he felt to be the pressure of rapidly moving times; finally he affirmed the drive towards freedom to be the indwelling of deity. That god is of another kind than the Creator and Redeemer confessed by traditional Christianity. It is a god that is "born" — made manifest to the world — through man's struggle to be himself, a free being. Like Hofmann, Kavanaugh envisages a force working within the universe and driving towards ever increasing freedom. When man allows this force to possess him, he is "saved" from being judged irrelevant to the cosmic process and from being cast into the outer darkness that is reserved for The Old. His freedom is what is called in Hegelian-Marxist terms "the recognition of necessity." And man's part in the work of salvation is his acceptance of his fate to swim with the evolutionary stream.

The freedom desired by Hofmann, Kavanaugh, and many more champions of liberation is one that knows no limitations at all. On the cosmic scale it is relative, certainly, for otherwise it could not keep going upward and onward. But every consciousness that surrenders itself to the irresistible force of freedom and moves with it can have no thought of proposing limited objectives, for fear of being thrown aside as deadwood by the ongoing cosmic force. Hence, the catch phrase "being open to the future" (often accompanied by the complementary phrase "and freed from bondage to the past") sets the mood in which expectations of increasing freedom are held. Under the influence of this mood the wildest hopes seem reasonable, and the dream of freedom can never be of less than absolute freedom. Indeed, to those who have had the vision of the archangel freedom drawing his sword against the enemies of progress, "to doubt would be impiety, to falter be a sin." And to think for a moment of asking where the archangel is taking us, and what his positive plans are when victory has been achieved, would be more than a mere mortal could presume. Our duty is to accept the role of agents of change in the contemporary world and to press on as befits loyal servants of the Great God Change. Inspired by the slogans and catchwords that constitute the holy scriptures dictated by the spirit of the age, we need know only that in the process we will be fulfilled and become "genuinely human."

Perhaps the following little dialogue has a moral.

Gadarene Swine A. Where are we going?

Gadarene Swine B. We are being liberated from the status quo. We are experiencing creative change. We are proving ourselves to be God's avant-garde.

A. Isn't that a cliff-edge ahead?

B. That isn't relevant. If you refuse to keep yourself open to the future you will never realize the full potentiality of contemporary swine-hood. Don't you want to fulfil yourself and exercise the choice by which you can become really swinish? Celebrate your freedom!

A. I think something's gotten into me, for my feet keep running, though I don't know why.

B. Don't slow down, or you'll be missing a genuinely meaningful experience. We've a message that truly speaks to our age, particularly since verbal communication has only brought alienation.

A. I can see the sea below. I wish my mother had taught me how to swim. Good-bye.

B. Don't worry. Love that sea, and *will* to sink beneath its waves. Through our embrace of casualty we choose life.

The Myth of the Invincible Young

Is such an image too extreme to illustrate one of the widely supported trends in today's world? Perhaps not, if we remember the ending of that remarkably percep-tive film *Dr. Strangelove*. How memorable the image of the Texan pilot falling and crying "Whoopee!" (as though to spur on the speed of his mount) as he sits astride the bomb that will activate the Russian Doomsday machine! It is an image of the same type as that of the swine driven over a cliff by a satanic spirit. This ending justifies the subtitle of the film: "How I Stopped Worrying and Learned to Love the Bomb." And, in cutting out before the inevitable impact, it follows the familiar pattern of the ending of many nightmares. It is commentary on the subconscious fears of a generation encouraged to believe in the dream of a universe evolving toward freedom.

The last sentence of the fictional dialogue above, at any rate, is not mine. It is the last sentence of the chapter "The Demand for Hope: Falling Casualty" in John Pair-man Brown's *Planet on Strike*. Again, we note the image of the fall placed in juxtaposition with hope — hope being here the equivalent of the pilot's "Whoopee!" But in Brown's imagination there is no irony. He says we *ought* to see falling casualty as a choice of *life*.

We have already quoted from *Planet on Strike* in con-nection with the argument that the abstract vision of life is a dream-vision that takes no account of the concrete realities which must be met. In a dream-world evolving toward freedom we should be able to behave as Brown asks us to, and issue a "non-negotiable demand for life." At least, that abstraction called the human race might do so. (Even while dreaming, very few real people would be so forgetful of the conditions of reality as to imagine that anything of the sort would be a sensible thing to attempt.)

Perhaps we should amend the "even while dreaming" in the preceding sentence to "even while drunk" in view of the following statement by Brown:

> The cracked leather of traditional institutions has a flexible new wineskin inside; the rising ferment of people's rebellion is the actual sap which must be poured into it. The young bear the future; revolution wins out in the end. . . . To avoid further bloodshed and stiffening of positions, the old must relinquish the power which in any case will be taken from them by death.[3]

This statement is an almost archetypal example of invoking the Perennial New in plain disregard of concrete facts. In this view a mythical entity called the young embodies the spirit of the new. A myth of the invincible young is then called on to prove that the dream of absolute freedom really applies to our history, so that revolution must win out at the end.

In fact, as many revolutions are lost as are won, and the revolutions that succeed either lapse from their original programs or are overthrown by counterrevolutions. Who knows what happens in the end? History is still going on. Meanwhile, on the strength of an abstract theory, it is argued that the old *must* relinquish their power gracefully and await patiently their fated extinction. Generalissimo Franco and Chairman Mao seem not to have heard of this law.

No real revolution is actually carried out by the young against the old. Riots on university campuses may give that impression. But riots are always between easily identifiable groups. In that respect, student-administration riots resemble convict-guard riots in prisons. Riots are not revolutions. Revolutions are carried out by revolutionary parties involving people of all ages. Young people, it is true, are usually the active shock troops in any revolutionary action. They are also the first to be disillusioned.[4] The young who are genuinely fired with revolutionary zeal are those who know a revolutionary regime only as

---

[3] *Planet on Strike*, p. 2.

[4] It was out of his experiences in the Spanish Civil War, where he fought for a "people's rebellion," that George Orwell wrote his "reactionary" novels *Animal Farm* and *1984*. Orwell's *1984* was favorite underground reading among young intellectuals in Czechoslovakia, which at the time had been recently "liberated."

the status quo; or who have never been through a revolution and see it as an abstract ideal. Most revolutions are initiated by the old (the theorists), led by the middle-aged or slightly younger (the activist soldiers and politicians), and afterwards maintained as a rigid Establishment by the Old Guard. So it is that most revolutions go from the old to the old.

Evidently Brown would maintain that "people's rebellion" is something entirely different from all this, something entirely unprecedented and unique — though it may have been heralded long ago by the revolutionary ideas of Jesus. A "people's rebellion" *is* different, of course. It is a mythical idea, a dream floating above and beyond the facts of history. Like a "People's Republic" it is an abstraction which is supposed to represent the distilled spirit of the people and which has no actual relation to the number of living persons actually filled with that spirit and agreeing with the accuracy of the name. If we ask for concrete evidence that there is in fact a people's rebellion, we will receive only the propaganda of those dedicated to maintain the myth intact. We are told that everyone supports what "the people" have freely willed — except, naturally, a few reactionaries, chauvinists, and other criminal elements.

To the slogan, "The young bear the future," the obvious reply is that they will have to grow old if they are to see any of it. One might also add that the less-than-young seem to coin most of the slogans. The myth of the invincible young seems especially attractive to those who are beginning to look back with nostalgia on their own lost youthfulness and think they can live vicariously in the coming generation.

Brown admits that he is a middle-aged person, but he says that he writes for the young. I am middle-aged, too, and I personally do not believe that the young are a special subsection of the human race that has to be written specifically *for* — as one might write *for* the mentally retarded or *for* those who will read nothing except pornography. The poet, said Sir Philip Sidney, comes "with

a tale which holdeth children from play, and old men
from the chimney corner." Surely every writer, knowing
that intelligence, imagination, and critical good sense are
not monopolized by any age group, would wish for the
widest range of readers possible. But since a larger per-
centage of the population than ever before is under thirty
years old, this group provides an obvious potential "market" for consumer goods, including indoctrinating reading
material. Spreading abroad the myth that the young are
invincible seems to me just as improper (to use no
harsher word) as spreading abroad the myth that the young
are decadent and irresponsible. Both myths encourage the
poor quality of imagination that goes with the stock
response. The former myth, however, includes an element
of flattery that assumes an intellectual and moral deficiency in its intended "market." This, I think, is more
insulting than the naked appeal to prejudice and fear in
the latter approach to its "market."

Traditional Christianity is assured that God's Providence
bears the future. Within that providential order, all who
are living bear their own share of responsibility for the
part they play in making the future better or worse than
it might have been. The young have no advantage over
the old; the old no privilege not shared by the young.
Individually, the young may well die before their elders,
even if collectively they will certainly outlast them. The
point is that none of us is indispensable, and each of us
is needed. The abstract categories of "the young" and
"the old" do not exist on the plane of history and can
play no part there.

Such abstract categories do have their uses. When
someone wants a tree climbed he does not usually send
for Grandpa, nor when he wants to remember the year of
that extra wet summer a few decades back does he ask
little Harry. In such areas of life it is sensible to speak
about "the young" and "the old." It is even possible to
generalize informatively — to say that the young are more
adventurous than the old, less wary of changes, and more
ready to experiment with different options. (Joseph Con-

rad's novel *Youth* is a good example of the use of such an informative generalization.) Even so, cliché phrases about "needing the fresh vision of youth" or "not to expect old heads on young shoulders" are almost as often refuted as confirmed in our actual experience.

What is completely nonsensical is the picture of "the young" or "the old" walking around through the centuries fulfilling their separate destinies of bearing the future or relinquishing their power. Individual young (or not-so-young) persons take over when their elders die; *the young* do not — except in rhetorical speeches where clichés masquerade in the dress of profound truths about life. Similarly, individual old persons retire. When one of them does so with stock phrases about "leaving the young to bear the future," it is fairly sure that either he has been forced to step down by moral blackmail or else he is secretly hoping that "young Robinson" (maybe aged around sixty) is going to make a mess of things.

The Controlling Myth of Nonhistorical Life

In the study of comparative mythology some myths are called controlling myths because they form a center around which a large number of lesser myths collect and become assimilated to the pattern of the dominant one. Most poems also are constructed around one controlling image. Religious myths are complex clusters of images, developed over a long time and woven into intricate patterns by the imagination of a culture. Contemporary myths are mostly far more simple, yet the same processes can be seen working to produce them also.

So far I have spoken chiefly about the "modern" myth of the Perennial New and suggested that the myth of the Invincible Young should be understood as a submyth. The Perennial New itself, however, depends on a prior belief in the image of the universe seen as the theater of constant and progressive change. That is why I have spoken of the god of modern (post-Cartesian) idolatry as the Great God

Change. It is becoming increasingly evident that behind the entire trend that has given us the cult of relevance, the worship of the Great God Change, and the quest for the promised land of liberation, lies an image that gives a definite shape to the trend. This is the image of "life."

The image is indifferent to life in the sense of actual existence — your life or mine — and thus is strictly non-historical. It takes its meaning from the image of organic life, which, we have seen, furnishes the basic image for Hegelian philosophy. To the extent to which the mechanistic image becomes less popular, the organic image and its ideal of the generalized life principle become more prominent. The mechanistic image is still very potent to stir stock responses (especially in the automobile form). Nevertheless, perhaps partly because of the recent publicity given to conservation of natural resources, the organic image seems to be gaining very rapidly in popularity and wide exposure. One sign of this is the change in emphasis observable in the idea of liberation.

At first liberation was an almost exclusively political concept. It is still often understood in political terms. As this is being written, we are reminded of this by news headlines about Vietnam, Bangladesh, Palestinian guerrillas, and the Irish Republican Army. By the time these words appear in print there may well be similar headlines about other places in the world where liberation is a war cry, and some of the countries mentioned may have been dropped from the news as quickly as happened to Hungary, Czechoslovakia, and Biafra. Until recently, secularizing Christians thought of liberation in political and social terms also, urging us to be aware of where God was at work in the world, liberating the captives. At that time the Secular City was the focus of attention, and we were called to celebrate its liberties. More recently the accent has been upon internal freedom.

Hans Hofmann, quoted at the beginning of this chapter, typifies the prevailing outlook: "In the final analysis freedom is basically a shifting of emphasis from the outside to the inside. When we begin to trust ourselves, we are well on our way to achieving freedom." [5] It might seem that this shift to inner experience in the quest for liberation has to do with the New Testament understanding of freedom as an inward grace not depending on outward circumstances but given with the knowledge of divine truth (John 8:32; Rom. 8:2). Certainly, the shift indicates a religious motivation and a decision to break away from the idea that only that freedom which is recognized by "the world" is legitimate in our age. The hope is now to find a liberating divinity at work in the soul of man. ("The soul" and "the divine" are no longer considered irrelevant, meaningless, dead words for contemporary man as they were in the sixties.) Yet the divinity supposed to be at work is still clearly the Great God Change. Man is the channel through which the god of the organic process carries on his work of perfecting life and liberating further evolutionary forms of life. That is the keynote of this variety of idolatrous belief.

If man's immediate consciousness or "soul" is where the Perennial New is perpetually coming to life, it follows that learning to trust ourselves is the first step toward liberation. The self-sufficiency of man is the beginning of freedom. Emerson said as much when he spoke of redemption as found in the Soul and required everyone to depend on his own consciousness of the indwelling divine and not on authorities old and dead. As though adding a footnote to Emerson, Hans Hofmann remarks that Buddha taught how enlightenment comes from within and not from outside. But, he adds, we must not simply trust Buddha or any other spiritual leader, for "man fulfills himself and his evolutionary mission only when he discovers for himself through experience the relevance of any insight or truth."[6]

[5] *Discovering Freedom*, p. 4.

[6] *Breakthrough to Life* (Boston: Beacon, 1969), p. 141. Hofmann often seems to echo Emerson. The following judgment upon the distance between the teaching of the Christian church and the "pure" teaching of Jesus is thoroughly Emersonian: "The Christians found it easier to worship a strange and unbelievable demi-god than to seek and unfold within and among themselves such Christ-consciousness" (*ibid.*), p. 214.

Kavanaugh puts the matter bluntly: "Man alone can save man; man alone will save man. . . . He will rely on himself."[7] Others are less direct. Harvey H. Pothoff suggests that man ought always to "take God into account." What does he mean?

> To take God into account in one's decision-making is to acknowledge the ultimate and cosmic significance of what it is to be a decision-making creature.[8]

In other words, if man makes up his mind and "takes God into account," he realizes that God himself cannot make up his mind for him. Therefore he sees his making up his mind to be a godlike act proving that any God outside his mind is completely redundant. Pothoff, in short, agrees with Emerson that man must always look within himself for direction. Presumably, he agrees also with Hofmann, who states that "the cornerstone of the Christian faith lies in its insistence that God fulfils his creative and redemptive life through man."[9] It does not require a great deal of perception to see that the God referred to is not the Creator and Redeemer, the God and Father of our Lord Jesus Christ, but the Great God Change. The "creative and redemptive life" of the god is seen in the Perennial New carried "through" man, since man is the channel of the evolving consciousness of the divine life.

"Life," of course, is a word central to almost all varieties of religious faith. Yet by no means does it always presuppose the same image. In the New Testament the many references to "life" and "eternal life" have the same significance: life is always personal life that finds its source in the personal living God. (In the Old Testament the phrase "As I live" denotes the personal assurance of the living God.) On the human side, this image of life gives rise to the question, "Good Master, what shall I do to win eternal life?" (Mark 10:17); or — since salvation is salva-

---

[7] *The Birth of God*, p. 103.

[8] *God and the Celebration of Life* (Chicago: Rand McNally, 1969), p. 257.

[9] *Breakthrough to Life*, p. 214.

tion *into life* — "Masters, what must I do to be saved?" (Acts 16:30). The question, we should note, is a personal one, addressed to an actual person or persons. Quite otherwise, the life offered by the Great God Change is offered to no individual, only to that abstract entity called Man.

If the image of nonpersonal life appropriate to Man is to be accepted, the image of personal life given to men by their Creator must be totally repudiated. Therefore, the first necessity in propagating the myth of the Perennial New is — as Hegel realized — to declare the Creator God dead. A personal God cannot be associated with abstract life: the image is wrong. The living God of traditional Christianity, then, must be declared a myth unacceptable to contemporary man. The decks are now cleared for the introduction of the new myth with its image of life, which is the impersonal life of a process. The life given by the Great God Change is a life belonging to all that participate in the process and to none. Man possesses it; men do not, except insofar as they lose their personal identity — literally — in the process.

A characteristic, if rather effusive, statement of the controlling myth of abstract life is given by Barry Wood in his book *The Magnificent Frolic*. Beginning with a chapter on "God's Death in Our Time," Wood goes on to describe life-as-process in the following terms:

> To understand the whole cosmos as "creating-destroying-res-urrecting" is to catch a vision of the most amazing spectacle there is — the panorama of life itself. "Resurrecting" is the visible process of day emerging out of night, spring rolling out of winter, living things growing out of the dead matter of their forerunners. The whole universe is one huge "destroying-creating" organism, rising like the imperishable phoenix out of the ashes of its own conflagration. . . .
> Life merges out of death, but it is not "this" life or "that" life, but life — or *living*. If the sacrifice of the divine in becoming flesh is *total*, how can man expect to sacrifice less? The life that emerges out of death is *new* life, unrecognized, even as Christ was unrecognized on the road to Emmaus. What

is meant by faith in the resurrection is faith in the ever-moving
flow of the "creating" process. Out of death life *must* come.[10]

Wood can advance his theory about the meaning of the
whole universe so confidently only because he assumes
the progressive-organic image to be unassailable. According to this image, Christ is simply a vegetation deity, and
his resurrection is a myth of spring rolling out of winter.
Yet Wood is not quite candid with us. Out of death life
must come? "Living" maybe — until the process is ended.
And there is certainly no guarantee of the immortality
of the world-process. But, in any case, all religious beliefs
that have sustained the hearts of men have begun precisely by facing the fact that living-in-the-process does
not mean this life or that life. No one on this earth can
speak for *life itself,* for no one knows what life is. Individual human beings, however, can and must speak for the
common life of men. No mountaintop, however lofty,
enables us to survey the cosmic process. The one place
where we are all *amazed* — in the original sense of that
word — is the place where we understand that, for us,
this life must end.

The Dance of Death

The view of life posited on the progressive-organic
image fates us to be the helpless victims of an abstract
and pitiless destroying-creating power. As far as we are
concerned, this power brings us into being purely in
order to destroy us. For us the "resurrecting" part of the
world-process is, as Wood reminds us (while remaining
apparently quite oblivious of the savagely ironic force of
this comment), out of our dead matter. In the ongoing
process we have no other function than to be forerunners
of *the new*. Thus are the grim features of the Great God
Change uncovered. This god offers us abstract life and

[10] *The Magnificent Frolic* (Philadelphia: Westminster, 1970), pp. 148,
149; italics in the text.

total freedom within the organism. Concretely, he offers us one certainty — death. He is the killer god.

Abstract delight in contemplating "the panorama of life itself" is not easily maintained when we remember that it is all the work of the killer god and that "resurrected" organic life feeds upon the mulch of decaying corpses. Even Hegel found it necessary to whip up enthusiasm for the image of the progressive-organic universe of absolute freedom by castigating the "insane presumption" of those who objected to giving up their individual freedom to submit to "nature's strict and holy necessity." There is, however, another way of becoming reconciled to the killer god and his kingdom of living death.

Every plant has its day, and putting out green leaves must bring it a great deal of satisfaction. It lives in the ecstasy of growth. That it must soon wither, or be killed suddenly by frost, or be trodden underfoot, or be cut down and put in a vase or a cooking pot — these contingencies lying in the future do not touch it now. Vegetable life, then, can be taken as the ideal for man. The vegetable image clearly underlies Charles Reich's *The Greening of America.* For what Reich calls Consciousness III, "life" is prior to all other considerations. We are to live as free as the flowers that bloom in the spring, and never even give a thought to the fall. *The fall,* as traditional Christianity images it, certainly has no place within Reich's imagination.

There is today a widespread return to the romantic preoccupation with nature, with its dream of a green and pleasant land so different from the man-made world of grid planning and concrete highways and urban congestion. This movement is one of the periodic "back to nature" calls heard ever since the "modern" age began and men started to control the world through science and technology. The concern for conservation of the earth's resources — which actually is a concern of scientists and technologists — has certainly been one factor in initiating the present romantic trend. But like everything else in this age of publicity and promotion of the stock response, it

has become a dream of a Never-Never Land popu-
lated by perpetually youthful Peter Pans. The hippies
of the 1960s saw themselves in the role of the new
breed of mankind that was to enter the promised land
of liberation from the ratrace of competitive industrial
society, materialism, and the profit motive. But they per-
ished at the ending of the dream in the squalors of Haight-
Ashbury. Now the dream is spread wider and more thinly.
It finds expression in the slogan, "Let It Be" (to be interpreted as "Let It Grow"), and in the universal popularity
of the vapid moralizing of *Desiderata* with its simplistic
message, "You are a child of the universe, no less than
the trees and the stars; you have a right to be here."

On the religious level there has been a return to anything that promises *immediate* consciousness of the divine:
drugs, divination, astrology, sensitivity and Esalen groups,
and oriental cults practicing meditation and ritual prayer.
Within the Christian orbit there has been an attempt —
seemingly rather successful — to propagate a "Dionysian
theology" both in the churches and around their fringes.

The Greek god Dionysus was a god of wine and sexual
energy, whose rites featured prominently ecstatic dancing.
Dancing is an image of natural growth. Its free yet strongly
rhythmic movements symbolize the life force that impels
both vegetable and animal to seek its full expression of
life. The ecstasy of the dance needs no justification beyond itself, while the dancers cease to be individuals as
they lose themselves in the spirit of the dance. Nietzsche
modeled his chosen ideal, the divine-man Zarathustra,
on Dionysus the dancing god. Now Sydney Carter's popular folk-hymn "Lord of the Dance" presents Christ in
the same image:

> *Dance, then, wherever you may be;*
> *I am the Lord of the Dance, said he.*
> *And I'll lead you all, wherever you may be,*
> *And I'll lead you all in the Dance, said he.*

In the Dionysian dance of organic life the promised land
of liberation seems to be in sight — more than that, actu-

ally to be enjoyed here and now. In an essay "Manifesto for a Dionysian Theology" Sam Keen explains:

> It may well be that in recovering a wondering openness to our total experience we may discover that ours is a holy place, that the events of our own personal histories tell a story of promise and fulfillment and give testimony to the presence of a power within human history which makes for wholeness and freedom.[11]

Yet it is not quite so easy as it seems, this promised liberation through the Dionysian dance. Keen quotes from Norman O. Brown:

> Dionysus, the mad god, breaks down the boundaries; releases the prisoners; abolishes repression; and abolishes the *principium individuationis,* substituting for it the unity of man and the unity of man with nature. In this age of schizophrenia, with the atom, the individual self, the boundaries disintegrating, there is, for those who would save our souls, the ego-psychologists, "The Problem of Identity." But the breakdown is to be made into a breakthrough; as Conrad said, in the destructive element immerse. The soul that we call our own is not a real one. The solution to the problem of identity is, get lost. Or as it says in the New Testament: "He that findeth his own psyche shall lose it, and he that loseth his psyche for my sake shall find it."[12]

So far as "our own personal histories" are concerned, therefore, we are back at square one on the board of the Great God Change's cosmic game. In order to join in the Dionysian dance of life we must lose ourselves completely in the dance and become one with "nature's strict and holy necessity."

Keen, it is true, does not want to go so far. He objects that Brown ignores "a crucial distinction between garden variety insanity and that divine madness which is the essence of creativity and joy."[13] Yet here Brown is quite consistent, while Keen wants to join the Dionysian dance

[11]*Transcendence,* ed. Herbert W. Richardson and Donald R. Cutler (Boston: Beacon, 1969), p. 51.

[12]*Ibid.,* pp. 40-41; from *Love's Body* (New York: Random House, 1966), p. 88.

[13]*Loc. cit.,* p. 41.

and at the same time refuse to acknowledge Dionysus as a real god. Certainly, Brown inexcusably misuses the New Testament text he quotes (Matt. 16:25), ignoring the personal reference to Jesus Christ, and supposing that the Dionysian unity of man with nature is the meaning of Christ's words. Yet Keen does not seem to object to that. And he might remember that Christ spoke about no servant being able to serve two masters (Matt. 6:24). If the Dionysian madness really is divine, and it requires the merging of the individual in the total organic process, then to maintain one's individual existence is to fall back into the *old* slavery, repression, and disunity with nature from which the god promises release.

Brown quotes from Joseph Conrad: "in the destructive element immerse." Conrad reproduces Buddhist teaching here; his meaning is that only by plunging into the unreal world of phenomena can one rise above it and know its unreality. Earlier I suggested that the image of the Gadarene swine was one image of which the age was aware, though unwilling to face directly. The sea-image, incidentally, is an almost universal one, found prominently in the Bible, for unconscious chaos. Contemporary man is widely being advised to immerse himself in the destructive element, to go down into the waters that destroy his individual existence, and to find courage for this self-destruction by first of all being filled with a spirit of madness. Nowhere is this advice more evident than in the invitation to join in the Dionysian dance. The dance of organic life is manifestly a dance of death.

Until the eighteenth century, a familiar image among Christians was that of the Dance of Death. Pictures of the dance, with Death as the macabre guide leading an assorted company of gay revellers, were often used by Christians to remind themselves of the truth that "life" — as those who knew only the energy and joy of organic nature thought of life — was the road to destruction. The only one who would call himself "The Lord of the Dance" was Death himself. Those who think to serve the Great God Change by following the Lord of the Dance, even if this Lord claims to be the true image of Jesus, will find that Dionysus is simply one of the forms this god assumes. And his *alter ego* is Death.

Idols That Make Men Blind

How has it been possible for the dance of death to have been mistaken for a dance of life and embraced with such enthusiasm? Why should the romantic dream of finding life by casting oneself onto the waters of unconsciousness and chaos have found so many willing dreamers today, except on the supposition of the old saying, "Whom Jupiter would destroy he first makes mad"?

Andrew M. Greeley, a Roman Catholic sociologist, has written about "the romanticism that swept through the American Church and indeed the whole American society in the last half of the 1950's, a romanticism that has increasingly become not merely anti-intellectual but irrational." He continues:

> Christianity without emotion and feeling is a perverted Christianity, just as science without emotion and feeling is a half-blind science. On the other hand, "Mind blowing," the anti-intellectualism, not to say irrationalism, of the current romantic binge, is profoundly disturbing to me. I think it is a good thing to let out the daemon within us, especially because the daemon is also a Ghost and a Spirit, but when man's rationality abdicates, his authentic daemon departs also, and what one has is not the daemonic, but all too frequently, the diabolic. . . .
>
> I suspect that the Dionysian turn both in the church and the larger society has the same motivation as did the Dionysian quest for ecstasy in ancient Greece — an escape from tragedy that is too much to bear, a running away from ugliness that is too horrendous to face.[14]

Greeley may be right. Escaping into the ecstasy of surrender to the immediate moment (and thus allowing the force of organic life to "dance" and obliterate the individual consciousness) is a welcome alternative to the sense

[14]*Come Blow Your Mind with Me* (Garden City, N.Y.: Doubleday, 1971), pp. 9-10.

of meaninglessness that comes from believing that one is a victim of an abstract cosmic destroying-creating process. The sense of movement, even though toward a plunge into the destroying waters, is much to be preferred to passive waiting for the juggernaut of the process to grind one into oblivion.

"In the destructive element immerse." There is a parallel here to the situation in the Greco-Roman world, when belief in the iron law of universal fate had removed hope from the human spirit. At that time, too, men turned to cults that promised to include them in the scheme of things. They found solace in the mystery cults, where they were initiated into immediate union with the cultic god; and to magical arts, where (as in the present turning to I Ching and the Tarot cards) they could obtain an intimate glimpse into the workings of fate.

There is another aspect also to the romantic binge, as Greeley calls it. This connects the irrationalism of Dionysian theology with the whole nature of idolatry.

In the Bible the devil is spoken of as the source of all falsehood. "When he tells a lie he is speaking his own language, for he is a liar and the father of lies" (John 8:44). All the powers that rebel against the living God likewise share this character, and those who worship them are both deceived and encouraged in self-deceit. Writing to the church at Rome, Paul says that idolaters have "bartered away the truth of God for the lie" (Rom. 1:25). The state of the person deceived by lies is spoken of in Scripture under the image of blindness. "Israel's watchmen are blind, all of them unaware" (Isa. 56:10) — these are the men who have to be told, "These idols of yours shall not help you when you cry; no idol shall save you" (Isa. 57:13). Paul writes about those who reject the gospel:

> Their unbelieving minds are so blinded by the god of this passing age, that the gospel of the glory of Christ, who is the very image of God, cannot dawn upon them and bring them light (II Cor. 4:4).

When the "imagination of men's hearts" is led astray by idols they are unable to know the "very image of God" when they see it. Having fashioned for themselves false images, they blindly follow a lie. The pervasive theme of this book is that the failure of the imagination to form images according to the revealed truth of the living God is the root of idolatry. And the half-truths encouraged by men's reliance on the stock response can lead to a more fatal blindness, a blindness in which "the god of this passing age" takes us away from the truth in the search for a supposed "relevance." It is not only that all belief in the living God and his saving word is made to seem "unbelievable" to "contemporary man." Even the distinction between truth and lying fancies is removed.

In the resultant misty twilight of the imagination, the most ordinary features of the world around us become hard to see clearly. The powers of critical intelligence languish, and common sense itself collapses into confusion. C. S. Lewis's *The Screwtape Letters* emphasizes this point repeatedly, presenting intellectual confusion as being central to the whole strategy of hell. "Keep everything hazy in his mind now," Lewis has a Senior Tempter advise a Junior, "and you will have all eternity wherein to amuse yourself by producing in him the peculiar kind of clarity which Hell affords."[15]

Idols that make men blind take care to call their gift of darkness by another name. "Enlightenment" used to be the popular term. Now it is more likely to be "insight into the human condition," or "a vision of the panorama of life itself," or "glimpsing the authentic shape of the future." The Great God Change is not likely to forget to

[15]*The Screwtape Letters* (New York: Macmillan, 1962), p. 13. The Senior Tempter Screwtape also tells his Junior Wormwood, "Jargon, not argument, is your best ally in keeping him from the Church. Don't waste time trying to make him think that materialism is *true!* Make him think it is strong, or stark, or courageous — that it is the philosophy of the future." "Do remember you are there to fuddle him. From the way some of you young fiends talk, anyone would suppose it was our job to *teach!*" (*ibid.*, pp. 8, 10). Although written over thirty years ago, *The Screwtape Letters* pillories much of the jargon presently considered to be contemporary — including, of course, the catchword *contemporary*.

promise that those who turn towards his shrine and worship him are turning towards the light. And should he be told that those who do so have difficulty in making out anything at all, he will be quick to reply that exposure to excess of light must be, for a short time, a blinding experience.

Death Is Not Life

A chapter on death in Hans Hofmann's *Breakthrough to Life* is prefaced by this quotation from Kahlil Gibran:

> If you would behold the spirit of death, open your heart wide unto the body of life. For life and death are one, even as the river and the sea are one.[16]

The idea that the truly liberated spirit will accept death as a part of life has quite commonly been exploited by those who image human life in organic terms. When they stress the sameness of the life force through all its manifestations rather than the variety that it produces, they frequently replace the vegetable image by the water image. Though water does not grow, the fact that it can flow and eddy produces the mood of ongoing life. And because separate drops of water seemingly merge effortlessly into an undifferentiated whole, the "unreality" of individual lives is suggested.

The assurance that those who use the water image would give, however, is exactly the one given to Eve by the serpent, "Of course you will not die" (Gen. 3:4). Still, at this stage in human history the universal experience of mankind can hardly be pushed aside without some attempt at an explanation. Men, most assuredly, imagine death to be real. So the answer is given, "You live, don't you? Very well then, life and death are the same. When you die, you are still living. Death serves life."

In the haze where death seems indistinguishable from

---

[16]P. 25; no source is given for the Gibran quotation.

life, it is overlooked that the assurance could equally well take this form:

> If you would behold the spirit of life, open your heart wide unto the body of death. For life is swallowed by death as the river is lost in the sea.

Moreover, insofar as men's efforts to build a community are concerned, the advice ought to run: "Steering your ship upon the rocks is the best way to emulate the river of life." The ecstatic Dionysian plunge into the destructive waters is the individual response to such advice.

Yet, even in a romantic haze, reality has a habit of breaking in. Greeley points out that the ancient and the modern cults of Dionysus have both had the same motivation: to shut out tragedy that cannot be faced. And traditional Christianity is more realistic by far when, instead of trying to palm off death as being equivalent to life, it calls death the last enemy to be abolished (I Cor. 15:26).

A favorite catch phrase of the worshipers of the Great God Change is "genuinely human." More genuinely human, surely, than Kahlil Gibran's affirmation of the unity of life and death is the speech Shakespeare gives young Claudio in *Measure for Measure*. In terror before his impending death, Claudio cries:

> Ay, but to die, and go we know not where;
> To lie in cold obstruction and to rot;
> This sensible warm notion to become
> A kneaded clod; and the delighted spirit
> To bathe in fiery floods, or to reside
> In thick-ribbed ice;
> To be imprison'd in the viewless winds,
> And blown with restless violence round about
> The pendant world; or to be worse than worst
> Of those that lawless and uncertain thoughts
> Imagine howling: 'tis too horrible!
> The weariest and most loathed worldly life
> That age, ache, penury and imprisonment
> Can lay on nature is a paradise
> To what we fear of death.
>
> (Act III, Scene i, 116-30)

Those who speak glibly of the unity of life and death would probably retort that Claudio is obviously an example of someone raised on superstitious myths. He is unable to understand that his "kneaded clod" is required by the destroying-creating organism to be the matter out of which it will resurrect new life. He does not understand that life, together with death, is a "magnificent frolic." Let him not think that "the selfish, nasty little egos men cling to and boast about and try to preserve are destined for everlasting life. . . . For the 'resurrecting' universe is a universe of harmonious flow where every day is a new dawn and every creation is a dramatic re-creation beyond belief."[17]

Claudio is admittedly a coward. But he is a man; and, if we dissociate ourselves from him through a Pharisaic sense of moral superiority, we repudiate our own humanity. Although some of the images of fear that he raises may take fanciful shapes, his basic image of death as a power utterly inimical to human life is truthful. His attitude to death is not Christian, as is that of his sister Isabella — who immediately whips him verbally for his cowardice and self-pity. Yet in his pitiable terror he speaks for all men, even for the most fearless. Claudio's vulnerable position saves him from the illusion of abstract thinking and romantic dreams.

The lying promises of the Great God Change may be believed in a romantic haze where truth does not seem to matter and the feelings of the moment cause the rational mind to abdicate. Total liberation through change may seem a plausible notion in an atmosphere where death is equated with life, evil with good, and thraldom to "sacred necessity" with freedom. But no amount of talk about "unbelievable myths" and a faith that is "not living for contemporary man" can postpone forever an encounter

---

[17] *The Magnificent Frolic*, p. 149, It is interesting to note how closely Barry Wood's remarks about "the selfish, nasty little egos . . . destined for everlasting life" parallel the remarks of Screwtape, who speaks about the appalling absurdity of God's wishing to "fill the universe with a lot of loathsome little replicas of Himself" (*The Screwtape Letters*, p. 38).

with the real world. Ultimately, idols are completely unbelievable because they are a lie. And in the real world
abstract images are just as powerless as graven images to
give us concrete aid against the powers that threaten us
as individual human beings.

When the living God calls men to himself by his saving
grace, he saves them with a power that is "beyond this
world," but he saves them in the world and not out of it
(John 17:15). By grace he calls them back into the real
world — the world that he has created — to understand
this world better than those who are "of the world." For
those who are "of the world" are under the power of
"the god of this world," a god who is an enemy of the
Creator's good creation.

It is no accident that one of the Hebrew words for an
idol is *atsab,* "a cause of grief." Grief is the reward for
the high hopes of all who seek to serve idols by putting
themselves in their power. "They worshipped their idols,
and were ensnared by them" (Ps. 106:36). The power of
idols lies in the dynamics of the nonexistent. This power
is actual enough, but it is always parasitic on the reality
that the living God has brought into existence. It continues only so long as he permits rebellion against his
perfect ordering of the world; and, so long as it continues,
it brings confusion to men's minds, false images to their
imaginations, and the overturning of all their dreams of
progress and community. Idols deceive men, constructing
a world of mere appearances, a world modeled on the
poor imagination that lives by the stock response. But the
living God rules over a world that is real and marvelous
in its variety and beauty and mystery. This is the world
inspiring the poetic imagination of men to discover ever
new and ever surprising images that reflect its truth. And
none of these images, however ancient they may be when
dated by the time of their discovery, can grow old or stale
insofar as they are a reflection of what is true.

Because the living God rules over a world that is real,
he too is the giver of real life — life in the world and

beyond it. The salvation that he offers is real, really issuing in freedom to live. In his service is perfect liberation.

> *Be at rest once more, my heart,*
> *For the LORD has showered gifts upon you.*
> *He has rescued me from death*
> *and my feet from stumbling.*
> *I will walk in the presence of the LORD*
> *in the land of the living.*

> (Ps. 116:7-9)

Part Three

Cleansing the Temple:
A Church Without Idolatry

7

To Turn from Idols

When Barnabas and Paul were at Lystra they were mistakenly identified with Jupiter and Mercury. They rushed into the crowd shouting their denials and affirming, "The good news we bring you tells you to turn from these follies to the living God" (Acts 14:15).

Turning from the worship of false gods is more difficult when those false gods have found their way into the Christian church itself. Quite early in the church's history the confusion caused by such an infiltration of idolatry was experienced. It was met by making clear the foundation of the Christian message in the truth of the living God himself.

> We know that the Son of God has come and given us understanding to know him who is real; indeed we are in him who is real, since we are in his Son Jesus Christ. This is the true God, this is eternal life. My children, be on the watch against false gods (I John 5:20-21).[1]

In every age Christians have to anchor themselves in the hope that the gospel offers (Heb. 6:19) and repossess the understanding of the living God given there. If our understanding is to be more than a repetition of phrases, it must

[1]See above, pp. 53-54.

131

involve our whole self. This means that our hearts, and "the imaginations of our hearts" as well, have to be focused on "him who is real."

The truth of the gospel is eternally the same, for it is the truth of Jesus Christ himself (Heb. 13:8). Yet in our interpretation of the gospel we are influenced, both consciously and unconsciously, by the various spirits abroad in the world today. There is no single spirit of the age to which we are bound, and the notion that there is, is a myth indicating the idolatrous worship of the Great God Change. If we are to turn from idols to serve the living God, we ought to be ready to recognize the forms of idolatry current in our midst. We ought especially to be alert to how these forms blind us to the truth of the gospel. By understanding how and where blind spots are likely to develop in our vision of reality we can be on guard against quenching the Holy Spirit when he seeks to open our hearts and minds to aspects of the truth that we are reluctant to admit. Only then shall we be enabled to swim against the stream of contemporary prejudices and false doctrines.

This section of the book, therefore, will consider how the idolatrous beliefs examined in Part Two impinge on our beliefs and practices within the fellowship of the Christian church. The present chapter is a kind of "hinge" chapter, staying with the general themes of Part Two, but showing how they are capable of being transformed within a Christian perspective. The following three chapters take up the subject of Christian worship and ministry, outlining how idolatrous tendencies can be met and overcome by a recovery of the living tradition of faith. There is undoubtedly a need to "cleanse the temple" of the Christian community by driving out the "spirits of error" (I John 4:6). At the same time, the house cannot be left unoccupied to invite the entry of other spirits of chaos (Matt. 12:43-45). Idolatry can be removed only by the positive appropriation of the resources known to faith in the living God.

From Relevance to the Wholeness of Truth

In discussing the irrelevance of relevance we noted that the concept of relevance cannot be informative unless it is very carefully qualified. There are at least three limiting questions that should be asked and answered before the assertion that something is irrelevant can be taken seriously: (1) relevant for what? (2) relevant for whom? and (3) relevant under what particular circumstances? Otherwise the judgment of irrelevance is no more than an ejaculation expressing prejudice — and arrogant prejudice at that.

When the notion of relevance or irrelevance is constructed into a general category and the blanket judgment is made that something or other is relevant or irrelevant, the notion usurps the place that properly belongs to truth. It is being said that something has (or lacks) value before any trouble is taken to inquire whether this something is fanciful or corresponds with reality. If it does indeed relate positively to reality, it may be quite true, and it must be at least partially true. If it is true at all, it is relevant. At least someone, somehow, somewhere needs to recognize the truth that it represents. And the liklihood is that, once its truth-content is appreciated, it will be found to be far more universally relevant than was previously suspected. If it is not true at all, of course, then the question of relevance or irrelevance cannot arise; it is a no-thing, not a something.

Take the case of a manufacturer and an environmental group who are clashing over the waste products from the factory that are being pumped into a nearby lake. The owner says the group's protest is irrelevant, since his factory supplies the only employment in the area. The group says that the owner's defense is irrelevant, since the one thing that matters is maintaining the environment. If employment is made the issue, the environmentalists argue, the coming of the factory has put an end to a previously thriving fishing industry. These two opposing sides can only insult each other until the facts of the nature and the extent of the damage caused by pollution are known. Then the possible steps required to prevent or contain the damage can be discovered, and action taken in the light of the total needs of the area. One of the parties — perhaps both — may have to retract or modify its position. Neither may be convinced that the right course has been taken in the end. Yet no other method of resolving the dispute is possible, whatever the outcome actually may be. Moreover, in our imperfect world the final decision is likely to be more on a basis of strong feeling (as reflected in the current anti-pollution laws, local "public opinion," exposure on the mass media, private lobbying, and so on) than on a dispassionate weighing of the available facts. But the issue is essentially one of truth; and the disputing parties' regard for, or disregard of, *what was real* will be that for which later inhabitants of the area will have reason to bless or curse them.

This example points to another disservice rendered by the cult of relevance. Truth cannot be compartmentalized. To investigate one issue is to open up others. There is a wholeness about truth that is not apparent unless one is willing to link up the partial truths presently known into a universal body of truth. Each problem solved points to other problems still unsolved; and the solving of these often means that unnoticed pieces of the earlier problems have to be looked at again, and the original solutions revised to make them more adequate. (The sciences provide numberless examples of this procedure, and philosophy is its classic embodiment.)

If relevance is absolutized, the wholeness of truth is a completely inconceivable idea, since the question of truth, even in a limited area, is deemed irrelevant. All that anyone needs to know is what is declared to be relevant for contemporary man by the Great God Change; and all that is relevant is given in the Perennial New. Relevance is asserted by repeating slogans and catchwords, thus arbitrarily ruling out any rational discussion of truth and falsehood, and bypassing by dogmatic pronouncement the delicate, exacting task of trying to examine an issue comprehensively and in its proper context.

In this connection, perhaps the greatest damage done to our sensibilities by the cult of relevance, through its encouragement of the stock response, is the success it has had in discouraging the historical imagination. Living in time, we depend on our memories to link one moment with another and so to find continuity in our experience. This is true for individuals. Each one of us learns through cumulative experience carried in our memory, so that lessons from the past help us to cope with the present and prepare for the future. It is also true for mankind. Whatever advance we may achieve collectively is gained by remembering what those who went before us have learned and by profiting from their experience. The quest for truth is a cooperative one, and cooperation between successive generations is one of its essential features. It is the historical imagination that makes this latter kind of cooperation possible. Previous generations leave us their experience, and, through the use of the historical imagination, we adapt their experience to fit our times and so to enlarge our own experience.

T. S. Eliot once wrote that we, of course, know more than the great men of the past whom we call the classics, for *they* are what we know. But it takes imaginative sympathy to know the classics. We lack that sympathy if our imaginations cannot conceive that the past has anything to teach us on the ground that contemporary man knows that the forms of the past are "not living" for us.

A few years ago, when the cult of relevance was at its height, thoughtful Christian teachers observed a disturbing phenomenon. Ministers and students attending conferences did not want to hear about the great theologians of the past or about the lessons of church history. "What is all this old stuff to us?" they complained. "Tell us about things that are relevant to us today. Today's world is different, and today's problems are unprecedented. We belong to a new age, and we have to speak meaningfully to contemporary man who just does not understand what all these old disputes were about. Besides, no one wants to hear about them when there are so many real, living issues to be faced right now."

Certainly, history that is divorced from the whole structure of truth can be arid. It was this kind of history that the Mouse in *Alice in Wonderland* recited when he tried (unsuccessfully) to dry Alice after her swim in the pool of her own tears, because, as he said, "This is the driest thing I know." But history for history's sake is precisely a refusal to exercise the historical imagination.[2] Nevertheless, what are we individually and collectively apart from our own past? What present being have we except that being which is sustained by the memories living through our imaginative reconstructions of the past? And, especially for Christians, what use is our common faith to us at the present time unless it be a story of events that we call to mind through a common confession of shared memories?

Christianity is an historical religion. Those who idolize relevance are always saying that we need to be set free from the dead past in order to be open to the present and ready to welcome the future hopefully. Yet, sunder any individual from his memory, and he is useless and helpless either to act or to plan for action. What we really need is to be set free from bondage to the present seen as an inescapable fate, and from fear of the future. Christian faith lives by the imaginative recital of events in the past. The great acts of the living God recorded in the Scriptures, which tell of how our salvation was won in historical time, are the events of the past that live in the memory of the

[2]C. S. Lewis directs a witty attack upon the "detached" Historical Point of View by making his fictional devil Screwtape praise it in these terms: "To regard the ancient writer as a possible source of knowledge — to anticipate that what he said could possibly modify your thoughts or your behaviour — this would be rejected as unutterably simple-minded. And since we cannot deceive the whole human race all the time, it is most important thus to cut every generation off from all others; for where learning makes a free commerce between the ages there is always the danger that the characteristic errors of one may be corrected by the characteristic truths of another. But, thanks be to Our Father [Satan] and the Historical Point of View, great scholars are now as little nourished by the past as the most ignorant mechanic who holds that 'history is bunk' " (*The Screwtape Letters*, p. 129).

Christian church. They must be shared by each Christian consciousness as believers draw on a common tradition in order to live in a common faith. "Many writers have undertaken to draw up an account of the events that have happened among us, following the traditions handed down to us by the original eyewitnesses and servants of the gospel" (Luke 1:1-2). This is how the early church sought to assist the continuance of the Christian "memory." The four Gospels themselves were written out of the memory of Christ's promise to his disciples that he and his words and acts would continue to live with them: "And be assured, I am with you always, to the end of time" (Matt. 28:20); and "I made thy name known to them, and will make it known, so that the love thou hadst for me may be in them, and I may be in them" (John 17:26).

The promise of the Lord of Christians has liberating power only if we remember what he did for us two thousand years ago in Galilee and in Jerusalem. The central act of Christian worship, the Lord's supper, focuses on his command, "This do in remembrance of me." Knowing through the Scriptures this living past that links us with our Christian beginnings, we are assured that nothing in it can be irrelevant and no part of it "incomprehensible to modern man." It is always a meaningful past that makes possible our imaginative perception of meaning in the present. The continuity of meaning also guarantees that what is now meaningful cannot lose its meaning at any time in the future. The men of the Old Testament trusted the living God to be with them through all "the chances and changes" of time:

> *The LORD will accomplish his purpose for me.*
> *Thy true love, O LORD, endures for ever;*
> *leave not thy work unfinished.*
> (Ps. 138:8-10)

Jesus Christ on the cross testified that the living God never leaves his work unfinished. There he said, of his own mission, which was also his Father's, "It is accomplished!" (John 19:30). And the apostolic witness to the mission of Jesus, on which the memory of the Christian church rests, affirms, "What we have seen and heard we declare to you, so that you and we together may share in a common life, that life which we share with the Father and his Son Jesus Christ" (I John 1:3).

Through the Christian memory we are led into the wholeness of truth, which is Christ himself.

From the Perennial New to Living Tradition

The cult of relevance holds that anything traditional is the acme of irrelevance. What is traditional is manifestly that which has not "kept pace." Tradition is the mark of the old, which is for slaves.

This stock response, making *tradition* into a dirty word, shows a lofty disregard for the wholeness of truth, and, more especially, contempt for the idea of wholeness achieved through continuity. For the existence of a tradition implies that there can be a continuity of truth maintained through the ages in different forms. Believers in any tradition stress the need for recognizable continuity. They recognize that people have to know and be prepared to confess their allegiance to the tradition in which they stand. But all traditions — though believed by relevance-idolaters to be rigid straitjackets — are flexible. Traditions do not stand still, but develop down the ages, not in the sense of getting better and better, but in the sense of finding new forms in which to express the truths that they stand for. Traditions do not progress; indeed, belief in inevitable progress is incompatible with the profession of belief in tradition. Neither the tradition of monarchy nor the tradition of democracy exhibits the same form today that it exhibited in ancient Sparta and Athens or even in England and the United States of two centuries ago. Neither the traditional orchestra nor traditional Christianity has remained exactly the same throughout its history or has yet reached the stage at which further development is impossible; for, had it done so, it would be a dead historical curiosity and not a living tradition.

All this is anathema to the worshipers of the Great God Change. Those who accept the myth of the Perennial New cannot accept the possibility of a living tradition, and therefore they speak disparagingly of "the dead hand of tradition" and of "the utter futility of applying traditional thinking to the totally new conditions of today." To admit the viability of a living and developing tradition, of course, would be to doubt the immutability of the Great God Change. The Perennial New cannot develop at all. The world-process expresses itself in the Perennial New, which is always encountered in its contemporary form; and all previous forms are to be dismissed as not living.

Those who acknowledge the validity of traditions, on the other hand, believe that truth can manifest itself in different forms. Because of this, they can admit the fact of change without making change into an idol. When they speak of a living tradition, their imaginations are not bound to the progressive-organic image of life. They realize that historical development is not the same as organic growth, even though the former may be in some respects similar to the latter. Thus they do not imagine that historical development necessarily means progress; and they do not deny, either, the possibility that something genuinely new can arise within the course of history. Because of their willingness to see what actually happens in history without trying to lay down the law about what "must" happen or what everyone living at the present historical moment "must" believe, they are able to accept both the old and the new. The new is not necessarily better than the old, and the old does not necessarily compete with the new. Nevertheless, in some areas of life and under some historical circumstances, the old has to give way to the new. It is as foolish to deny the possibility of limited progress as it is to affirm that inevitable progress is the basic law of the universe.

A useful illustration in this connection is the way that traditional Christianity identifies sacred Scripture with both the Old and New Testaments. Quite early in the history of the Christian church there appeared believers in the Perennial New, who were sure that the new message of Jesus had abolished the old message of Moses and the prophets of Israel. The best known of these champions of the new was Marcion, a teacher who supported his position by appealing to Paul's struggle with the Judaizing party who insisted on binding Christians to full obedience to the Mosaic law. Marcion's views were rejected on the ground that they broke continuity with the apostolic tradition. The Apostles had accepted the Old Testament as a true revelation of God, though one made old by the arrival of the new revelation in Jesus Christ. The new need not abolish the old. Marcion's teaching, however, introduced one feature utterly at variance with the teaching of the Apostles (including Paul), for it claimed that the God whom Jesus revealed was another God altogether from the God of Israel, who was a false god and the enemy of the God of Jesus. It was not the newness of Marcion's teaching that made it unacceptable: the idea of the rival gods was an old idea long current in Gnosticism. But Marcion misunderstood the truth of the gospel. What he said could not be reconciled with the new revelation, a revelation that contained the saying of Jesus, "When, therefore, a teacher of the law has become a learner in the kingdom of Heaven, he is like a householder who can produce from his store both the new and the old" (Matt. 13:52).

Both the new and the old — this is a statement applicable not to traditional Christianity alone but also to the whole approach to historical existence that recognizes the value of traditions for maintaining openness to the truth.[3] Once again, we should note that the historical approach to life does not absolutize any form of truth or any abstract principle. It does not deify tradition. Christians in particular should remember not to do so, in view of

[3]See also my *What's New in Religion? A Critical Study of New Theology, New Morality and Secular Christianity* (Grand Rapids: Eerdmans, 1968), especially Chapters 2 and 11-14.

Jesus' words to the Pharisees and lawyers, who idolized tradition (Matt. 15:1-9). Although the history of the Christian church shows that Christ's warning has been often forgotten, so that idolatry of tradition is part of the sorry record of denominational feuding through the centuries, this evil came about because Christians have so often forgotten the tradition that Scripture tells them to receive (II Thess. 2:15). A tradition beginning to deify itself is on the way to losing its life rather than being a carrier of the spirit of freedom.

Just as continuity means life, so tradition — which is continuity in structures or in patterns of thinking or in both of these together — means living freedom. Such a notion may be difficult to digest at a time when tradition has long had such a bad press that the stock response to it is one suggesting irrelevance, constriction, and hostility to the new. But one of the functions of tradition is to prevent stock responses from so dominating men's imaginations that the outlines of their images become blurred, and the quality of both their imaginative understanding and their conceptual thinking deteriorates.

When such deterioration sets in, people start to be incapable of pursuing the truth intelligently. They are ruled by stimuli from outside rather than by decisions they have made. Of course, one of the stimuli they will react to automatically is likely to be the slogan, "Don't be the slave of tradition — dare to think for yourself!" But thinking for oneself is literally impossible, if by that is meant behaving as if no one had ever done any thinking before and one is to begin *de novo,* starting from scratch. To begin with, one inherits a particular language-tradition, and that already gives him most of his images and thus does much to shape how he thinks. Furthermore, even when we imagine we are inspired with some wholly original thought, we cannot totally forget everything we have heard said since our childhood. The chances are that our "creation" is an echo of something which we have heard or read and which has merely slipped into our subconscious mind.

In the seventeenth century Descartes made a valiant effort to begin thinking by dismissing every preconceived notion from his head. He was a genius with a disciplined mind, so that the result was indeed a new direction for philosophical thinking. Yet if we look back on his "new beginning," we can see how much he had absorbed, all unconsciously, from the mental atmosphere of his times. Descartes was successful in giving philosophy a push into a new track because he belonged to a living tradition, drew from that tradition, and contributed to it by looking at the actual world around him with the directness that the philosophical tradition demanded but which few previous philosophers had managed to achieve. Also, Descartes' success was largely the result of the fact that, in seeking the wholeness of truth, he had seen how the mathematical tradition could be merged with the philosophical to the advancement of both.

From Catchword-Dogmatism to Reverence for Truth

The evidence that a living tradition means living freedom is to be found in how people defend their opinions. Those who live by stock responses will argue if the slogans they repeat are challenged. Invariably, however, their train of reasoning turns out to begin in yet another slogan. Even where a fairly extensive and sophisticated rational justification is undertaken, the slogan-monger gives himself away by his sweeping judgments. Anyone who cannot actually imagine any other frame of mind than the one to which he himself has been conditioned will also usually imagine that any opinion which contradicts his own is not so much stupid as wicked. And so he will set forth his argument in a form that makes it quite clear that no other view will be permitted to exist. The dogmatism of the catchword-user has already been mentioned.[4] The dogmatic form of the following statements is unmistakable:

[4]See above, pp. 71-74, 100.

"No truly contemporary person can . . ."

"Anyone who expects to be taken seriously today must . . ."

"No other . . . has the slightest hope of success in an age such as ours."

"Unless you wish to be entirely irrelevant . . ."

"In order to have any future at all, religion must . . ."

"The future lies with those, and only those, who . . ."

"Man is learning, in our unique age, to . . . and at the same time he is turning away from . . ."

Sentences such as these are scattered all around us. (I found all of these in the space of a few minutes, while leafing through half-a-dozen theological books and journals.) Each makes a categorical affirmation, and some carry a direct threat as well: "If you won't accept my word for it and do what I say, I can't be held responsible for the consequences!" It is interesting how frequently the future is held up as a bogey-man to frighten bad children who will not toe some party-line or other without question. Of course, for worshipers of the Great God Change the most dreadful fate possible is being left behind in the old when the Perennial New moves on to a new form. They fear most of all being thrown on the scrapheap of the evolutionary process.

Those who believe in tradition have no such fear, and so they do not need to have recourse to catchword-dogmatism. This does not mean that they have no definite convictions, or that they believe that anything goes because everything is relative. Every tradition has its roll of martyrs, men who thought the living tradition in which they stood to count more than their individual lives. But people who honor tradition know very well that their own tradition is not the only one possible. Although they may think that those who reject that tradition are mistaken, they are aware that other options are possible.

Equally, they are aware that the tradition to which they have given their allegiance is not perfect in its present form; and thus that no one now living can tell his fellows precisely what they must believe, or dictate what is and is not possible for contemporary man, or announce the shape of the future. A living tradition is authoritative. One cannot depart from the mainstream of any tradition and still claim to belong to it. But it is not authoritarian, in the sense that it demands acceptance of a party-line without question. A living tradition is alive because it can be changed in any of its expressions that do not involve a loss of true continuity. *Ecclesia semper reformanda* — the church stands in need of continual reformation — that is a typical statement of the tradition-honoring point of view. And the line between changing traditional forms (interpreting the tradition for today) and breaking continuity so as to lose touch with the whole tradition is a line that cannot be drawn *a priori*. There must always be room for discussion, and even the admission of difference of opinion that cannot be reconciled at the present moment. All traditions split into separate parties, some of which go their own way after breaking fellowship with the rest. Yet, so long as the tradition is not wholly lost because of party strife, there is always hope that the different strands of the tradition may yet unite again in a more complete expression of the tradition which each seeks to uphold in its own fashion.

Someone may object that, in point of fact, many traditions are dogmatic, intolerant, and contemptuous of opposing views. Yet this realization is itself part of the tradition-honoring outlook. Men can make anything into an idol, including tradition. Nevertheless, the use of a thing is not shown in its abuse. Whereas the worship of the Great God Change cannot by its very nature tolerate rival views, honoring tradition does not mean raising it to the status of a god. Every tradition seeks to embody some truth, though it will not be able to embody this truth perfectly in an imperfect world. The command that tradition-honoring people obey is, "Keep the tradition, and hand it on at least as well preserved as when you received it." This command is exemplified in the Christian tradition by Paul's warnings against preaching "another gospel" (II Cor. 11:4; Gal. 1:6). But to keep the faith does not mean keeping everything exactly as it was. Here again, the theme is that the old and the new can be partners instead of implacable enemies. That the inheritors of a tradition will sometimes fight instead of cooperate is a fact of life: it must be admitted, but it need not be consented to despairingly. To despair of living tradition is to despair that the voice of truth can make itself heard on earth among the noisy slogans of the self-opinionated. Such despair is, among those who honor tradition, the final apostasy. Those who belong to a tradition are its stewards, and faithfulness is required of stewards (I Cor. 4:2).

Faithfulness is not the same as blind obedience. It is something very different, namely, confident and discriminating obedience. In the early Christian church faithfulness in the face of circumstances that made for despair was seen as the final test of obedience. So it was said that the blood of the martyrs was the seed of the church. At the same time, the rule of the church was that no one had the right to make himself a martyr unless circumstances left him with no other choice. A tradition reveres the truth and believes that the truth is worth more than existence without it. But it claims ultimate loyalty not for itself but for that which it embodies.

Thus tradition is never honored as an end in itself, but because it exists to promote reverence for truth. Here we can see why honoring a tradition leads away from reliance on stock responses and promotes flexibility and breadth in the imaginative vision. When it may seem to be most dogmatic, the mind that honors tradition retains its humility before the truth and a sense of its own inadequacy to state any truth fully and accurately. This is because it knows that any single consciousness grasps no more than certain aspects of that tradition which it honors; and also because it knows that the tradition itself, in its presently existing form, does not possess the truth entire but can only strive to keep itself open to the truth.

Take, for example, the quoting of Scripture in the Christian tradition. Admittedly, Scripture may be misused.

It is misused when verses are torn from context to serve as prooftexts for a dogmatic framework imposed on Scripture instead of drawn from it. To a certain extent, too, the most conscientious user of Scripture can never be completely certain that all his references to Bible verses reflect the biblical message and have not been distorted to support some theory of his own invention. But, when Scripture is quoted faithfully, the silent comment is always implied, "If I have misused Scripture, let others within the tradition correct my errors." Moreover, the reason for quoting an individual verse or passage of the Bible is always the same. It is that an individual may make clear that he is giving more than a private opinion. In fear and trembling, he dares to speak for the tradition to which he belongs. He lays claim to a wisdom deeper than his own thinking and to a store of images wider than his own imaginative reach. He does this, not to display his own cleverness, but out of reverence for the truth.

From Abstract Liberation to Personal Freedom

The visible line between humble reverence for truth and a proud claim to possess it may be very thin. Yet this indicates the importance of a man's being fully aware of the tradition in which he stands. Worshipers of the Great God Change commonly ignore that they belong to an identifiable tradition that has long existed as a rival to "traditional Christianity." Since "tradition" is a wicked word in their vocabulary, they prefer to say that they are "facing the unprecedented challenge of our age" or trying "to stimulate theological thinking in a new direction."

This last phrase is Barry Wood's. In *The Magnificent Frolic,* he attacks "traditional theology" for not understanding that the "Exalted Man" (the Ascended Christ) refers to *all* men. After quoting from Athanasius, "He became man that we might become God," Wood writes:

And here the meaning of Easter — Ascension and Pentecost —

breaks out of the realm of the "historical" event and into the realm of that timelessness which is eternity, since the birth of the Spirit in man is the *real*-izing or dis-covering of the Spirit that has been within man from the beginning. For the Spirit of man is God's breath, the *ruach Adonai* that was breathed into the first Adam when "man became a living being" (Gen. 2:7).[5]

This part, at least, of the "new direction" for theology was well known to John Calvin, who wrote:

> But before I proceed farther, it is necessary to advert to the dream of the Manichees, which Servetus has attempted in our day to revive. Because it is said that God breathed into man's nostrils the breath of life (Gen. 2:7), they thought that the soul was a transmission of the substance of God; as if some portion of the boundless divinity had passed into man. It cannot take long time to show how many gross and foul absurdities this devilish error carries in its train *(Institutes,* I, xv, 5).

Moreover, this same new direction was familiar to Athanasius. Many of his writings against the Arians were devoted to refuting their contention that biblical language breaks out of the realm of the historical event into an eternal realm of timelessness. Wood's reference to Athanasius, therefore, involves misusing the Greek Father's concept of *theosis* (deification); and his reference to Genesis involves forcing biblical language into the mold of the dogmas of a Gnostic-docetic theology. Had Wood simply said that he greatly preferred the Gnostic tradition to the tradition of the Apostles and the church fathers and the Reformers, and that he was adopting that tradition as it had been appropriated in the Hegelian theology of the progressive-organic process, we should know where he stood and we stood.

Ignoring traditions means confusing them — and thus confusing ourselves. Wood, for example, is delighted to find that the theology of Hinduism supports his gnosticized Christianity. From this he concludes that the Bible "really" teaches liberation from the temporal through the divine breath of life breathed into man. He writes:

[5] *The Magnificent Frolic,* p. 154.

> The Spirit of God (Brahman) is therefore the spirit of man (Atman). In the final Biblical and Upanishadic doctrine of God (the 'indwelling' Spirit and Atman-Brahman) is revealed the *philosophia perennis*, the final truth of all religion and all advanced science: that the deepest dimension of man is one with the deepest dimension of the whole universe.[6]

Wood not only declares his "new direction" in theology to be the final truth of all religion and all science. He adds "that it is the most undogmatic theology possible. . . . This is the theology of experience."[7] The experience which he appeals to is that of each human spirit being Vishnu in a million masks and treading through the universe without fear. "For this is a 'resurrecting' universe, and if I die I can be sure the universe will 'I' itself again and again and again."[8]

Obviously, no one actually experiences himself as one of the million masks of Vishnu dreaming the universe. If this be the final truth, only dogma makes it so. Yet, according to Wood's reasoning, one system of dogma suddenly becomes undogmatic, finally true, and a theology of pure experience. Could dogmatism be taken further? Perhaps it could, for Wood makes clear that a *creating* universe does not need a Creator, and that the living God of traditional Christianity is the Big Ego "of a bygone era" and also the Big Tyrant.

Abstract liberation is the promise of life through the gift of the Great God Change who, like Marcion's god, is the enemy of the tyrant Creator-God. The god can fulfil his promise only by giving a life that is nobody's life and that means everybody's death. The promise that the whole process will repeat itself again and again and again avoids the question of whether going through the "dream" at all is worthwhile, even for the privilege of knowing oneself to be Vishnu in one of his million masks. Abolishing the human ego together with the Big Ego is, as I have already

[6]*Ibid.*, p. 189.
[7]*Ibid.*, p. 203.
[8]*Ibid.*, pp. 195-96.

argued, to enthrone death as the ruler of the universe, the executive archangel (and chief executioner) of the Great God Change.

The abstraction called liberation conceives freedom in terms of unlimited sameness. This follows from the deification of change. Such an idolatry pronounces the dogma of the unreal creation. Historical existence is a dream, indeed, *the* dream from which finally true religion seeks to be delivered. There are no real individuals around, only masks of Vishnu-Spirit. The enemy of abstract freedom — the freedom to die in order to be "resurrected" and dream again and again and again — is the Other in all its forms. Therefore, the Great Other, the Creator who stands over against his creation, is the one who must at all costs be declared dead. Less is said about the Little Others, our fellow men; yet, they too are pronounced to be "selfish little egos" who have no right to life until they learn that their only reality lies in their inner identity with all-pervading Spirit.

More than a hundred years ago Søren Kierkegaard attacked the panspiritism of Hegel in the name of traditional Christianity. The spearhead of his attack was his assertion of the reality of the individual before God, that is, the belief that the Great Other created Little Others who could know him in freedom. From this belief follow many others. First, the biblical account of man and his creation is no myth to be demythologized in terms of a nontemporal and impersonal Spirit that is dreaming the world-process. No, the latter is the myth, a product of the abstract imagination rejecting concrete actuality. Second, myth is idolatrously preferred to actuality, because it promises an easy escape from the complex demands of daily existence by simple "breakthrough" into timeless sameness. Third, the abstract dream of total liberation is contradicted every moment by the existence of other selves. Therefore, the principle of individuation has to be denied, and the ego downgraded as the product of selfish illusion. Fourth, in relationship is found the freedom that individual existents can enjoy. But relationships limit the self while enlarging it, and thus the world of relationships is seen by the abstract imagination as a world of slavery from which we can escape by sinking ourselves in the timeless sameness of identity with Spirit. Since a God who is Spirit and also the Creator has created us for relationship with himself and with our fellows, this living God must be declared to be a projection of ourselves, and the biblical statement that *we* are created in *his* image rejected as a myth. The individual before God, caricatured by the idolatrous imagination as the selfish little ego cowering before the Big-Ego Tyrant, is precisely in the relationship which Scripture declares to the freedom given by knowing the truth. "If you dwell with the revelation I have brought you, you are indeed my disciples; you shall know the truth, and the truth will set you free" (John 8:13-32).

Christ is not abstract humanity. He came in the flesh, an individual man, Jesus of Nazareth, who was also the only Son of the Father. Our freedom comes, not by plunging ourselves into the world-process and losing our individual selves in the stream of organic life, but by becoming the selves which the living God created us to be by responding to this individual Person. In the relationship of the Kingdom, we find our freedom. "The slave has no permanent standing in the household, but the son belongs to it for ever. If then the Son sets you free, you will indeed be free" (John 8:35-36).

From Death-Ecstasy to Eternal Life

One area of life in which liberation is eagerly sought is the area of sexual experience. In the notion of liberation through the sex act the equation of life with death is very obvious. Hans Hofmann, convinced that life and death are one, points out an historic image linking death and sex. Until the eighteenth century "dying" was a common name for sexual intercourse. Hofmann attributes the loss of this usage to "the repressive attitude toward sex which the Puritan middle class succeeded in foisting upon us." He adds that the usage still is not wholly lost "despite society's efforts to repress the notion that sex, as dying, can be a breakthrough into a new life."[9]

Where death is seen as a breakthrough to the abstract liberation of the organic life process, it is overlooked that sexual intercourse possesses (though it is not all that it possesses for those who value existence) the characteristics of the Dionysian dance. Sexual ecstasy gives the sense of plunging into the waters of unconsciousness and of losing one's individuality and becoming simply a channel for the destroying-creating life force. It is no accident that the *sacredness* of sexual expression was one of the great discoveries of the Romantic Movement of the early nineteenth century, and that in this romantic tradition "*falling in love*" was elevated to the position of the highest human value. For romantics, then and now, a love that is *fated* and not *willed* is assumed to be the only kind of love worthy of the name.

A more accurate way of speaking, of course, would be to say that the Romantics *re*-discovered the very ancient tradition which understood the sex act as a sacred ritual symbolizing the unending cycle of organic growth in vegetable nature that perpetually dies to make new life possible. The practice of ritual prostitution among the Canaanite neighbors of Israel gave rise to the images of fornication and adultery, which are the normative words in the Old Testament to describe idolatry. Among the Romantics, however, the social dimension of the ritual sex act was dropped. The meaning of the act was no longer to guarantee good harvests but instead to overcome the sense of alienation in the human spirit. Because anything *other* had become the enemy of life-seeking-liberation, sexual union promised a blending of flesh that, by plunging two individuals into the waters of oblivion, would allow the inner spirit in each to be "resurrected" as one true manifestation of spirit. In the Romantic vision there lived again the ancient gnostic belief that in sexual experience the

[9]*Breakthrough to Life*, pp. 43, 44.

masculine soul discovers its feminine counterpart and overcomes the division made by the tyrant Creator when he imprisoned pure spirits in flesh.

It was probably the Romantics, too, not the repressive Puritans, who caused the sexual sense of "dying" to drop out of currency.[10] The Romantics repressed the word, because love must be identified only with life at its most ecstatic, living intensity. But then they displaced the connection between sex and death to the point that the Other — in this case the Puritanical world, conventional society, or traditional Christianity's hatred of free spirits — could be blamed for it. In all the great Romantic love stories one or both of the lovers die, victims to society's "hypocrisy." They do so voluntarily, of course, usually by a suicide pact, but sometimes driven by the very force of their love to destroy each other's bodies, so that the Spirit of their love may live uncontaminated by the flesh. The latter outcome is shown in the most famous of the Romantic love stories, Prosper Mérimée's *Carmen*. Less free-spirited Romantics have one of the lovers die because of a fatal (fated) illness. The great success of Erich Segal's *Love Story* shows that this slow-death formula still has great popular appeal. But, while low-brow imaginations die sweetly with the *Love Story* type of death-in-life experience, high-brow imaginations prefer the bolder approach, as exploited for example in the film *Elvira Madigan*. There the lover shoots his mistress to preserve her in timeless life — shown on the screen by a prolonged "still" pose. In real life, too, Marilyn Monroe became assured by her suicide of "immortality" as a true sex goddess.

Sex is still regarded in the Romantic fashion and taken

---

[10]Puritans, of course, are blamed for everything repressive, that is, not liberating. What the historical Puritans actually said or did is irrelevant, because Puritanism is not an historical label but a catchword guaranteed to raise a stock response. Screwtape says, "and may I remark in passing that the value we have given to that word ["Puritanism"] is one of the really solid triumphs of the last hundred years? By it we rescue annually thousands of humans from temperance, chastity, and sobriety of life" (*The Screwtape Letters*, p. 47).

to be an absolute value. As one writer has commented, "It seems to be the one green thing in an iron world." The promise of Dionysus is accepted automatically by thousands of his worshipers, who hear him say, "The solution to the identity crisis is: get lost — die in the sex act." Surrender to the "fate" of sexual love is seen as the achievement of absolute liberation. Meanwhile, sexuality seems to be losing its "greenness." Increasingly it is becoming impersonal and lacking in human meaning. As manuals on techniques multiply, sexual maladjustment and frustration seem to multiply likewise. As the opportunity for unlimited sexual experience increases, the possibility that an individual person can find joy and fulfilment through his sexuality seems to become ever more remote and problematic.

Christian faith affirms human sexuality as a joyous and a freedom-giving reality. But it also sees it as a responsibility, not as a plunge into unlimited liberation. Because we are sexual persons, we are more than incidental expressions of an impersonal life force. We are capable of entering into all the relationships that our sexuality opens up for us. We are not lovers only, for we can be also spouses, parents, children, uncles or aunts, nephews or nieces, cousins. Our sexuality finds its full expression, therefore, in the marriage bond and in all the human relationships that follow from this sexual — and properly human — relationship.

In the New Testament marriage is the image used to symbolize the relationship existing between Christ and the church (John 3:29; Eph. 5:22-33). No other image could so perfectly represent the community of life to which we are called. As husband and wife are joined not by mere biological necessity but by a fully personal relationship of mutual trust and cooperation, so the Christian community is united to Christ. As human marriage is a life bond, so in being united to Christ we share the gift God bestows in Christ — eternal life.

The biblical message about life and death is that the living God created man for life, but through man's sin death came into the world. No ecstatic plunge into death can resurrect a humankind subject to death. Death awaits each of us so long as the rulers of this present age retain their power. Nevertheless, through his death and resurrection, Jesus Christ has broken this power for those who believe in him. His words to us are: "I am the resurrection and the life. If a man has faith in me, even though he die, he shall come to life; and no one who is alive and has faith shall ever die. Do you believe this?" (John 11:25, 26). Eternal life is the promise given to believers. "And this is eternal life: to know thee who alone art truly God, and Jesus Christ whom thou has sent" (John 17:3). "As in Adam all men die, so in Christ all will be brought to life" (I Cor. 15:22). The promise does not offer any escape from individual existence in order to cheat the rule of death to which our sin has enslaved us. Eternal life is no death-is-really-life formula, no juggling with words making death appear to be a liberation of our "spiritual" being. Eternal life goes beyond death because the power of the resurrection of the Son of God has given us freedom to live beyond death.

The plunge into the destructive waters of death is indeed symbolized for Christians in the sacrament of baptism. Yet the symbolism of baptism is at the furthest remove from identifying death with life. The sacrament signifying our incorporation into Christ asks us to remember how the abstract power of death has been overcome by the personal, living power of the Christ of God. "Have you forgotten that when we were baptized into union with Christ Jesus we were baptized into his death? By baptism we were buried with him, and lay dead, in order that, as Christ was raised from the dead in the splendour of the Father, so also we might set our feet upon the new path of life" (Rom. 6:3-4). Christian faith does not ask us to lose our identity by immersing ourselves in the destructive element, but instead to find it by dying to ourselves and by rising with Christ. The triumphant expression of the Christian life is, "By gifts of the Holy Spirit, by sincere

love, by declaring the truth, by the power of God . . .
dying we still live on" (II Cor. 6:6-7, 9).

From Meaninglessness to the Communicating Word

One of the features of the worship of the Great God
Change is the compulsion it lays on worshipers of the god
to write off whole areas of existence as meaningless. We
are assured that the past is dead and so can have nothing
to say to us, that traditional language conveys nothing to
contemporary man, that God-talk is unintelligible and
secular language alone can be understood, and even that
words themselves are inadequate vehicles for communicating living reality.

This last contention is particularly sweeping, because,
if taken seriously, it would strike at the root of all human
communication. The ability to use language is the most
evident characteristic of *homo sapiens*. There is no race
of men that does not exhibit it, and the development of
civilization has gone hand in hand with the development
of language, both spoken and written, as an increasingly
flexible and complex means of exploring and sharing the
human experience of the world. When words are taken
to be obstacles to communication rather than mankind's
means of communication *par excellence,* what is often
referred to as "the present crisis in communication" has
indeed reached a danger point.

The view that verbalization is a source of alienation is
closely connected with the flight from personal existence.
It goes with the belief that humanity can be united only
by reversing individuation and returning to a preconscious
state of corporate unity. Thus, exponents of the Dionysian
dance are prominent among those who wish to downgrade
the function of words. For example, Sam Keen writes:

> That our age is post-Reformation means that it no longer hears
> the word of God with the ear of faith. The sacred must be
> rediscovered in what moves and touches us.
. . . .

The time is ripe to return to the primitive, the primal, the carnal. To repeat Darby Nock, "Primitive religion is not believed. It is danced." Words, concepts, doctrines, ideas are all very necessary for clarity and for consistent action. There is a time for words. It has lasted from the Reformation to the present. Now we are sick of being inundated in an ocean of verbiage. The word must be rediscovered in the flesh. Religion must return to dance.[11]

Now, hearing is what makes us most fully aware of the other. If we were limited to the sense of touch and seeing only, we might understand other people and things that came within our consciousness as no more than extensions of ourselves. The testimony of Helen Keller, for example, makes abundantly clear that the awakening to consciousness of the function of language is the door through which we must pass if we are to become individuals in our own right; and that even being deprived of the physical basis for hearing sounds need not prevent us from "hearing" human speech.

Keen's dogmatic claim that we are living in a post-Reformation age is a variant on the theme of the irrelevance of traditional Christianity. Assuredly, the Reformation did not invent the image of hearing the word. The Reformers were simply anxious to stress one element in traditional Christianity that they felt had been unduly overlaid by other and less important elements. The image of hearing the word came to them through medieval Christianity from its roots in the Old and the New Testaments. If we are talking about "a time for words" more generally, there is no doubt at all that this time is coextensive with the entire history of the human race. There is no scrap of evidence that the age-old tradition of human speech has reached its end and is no longer needed. Wordless ecstasy is not yet the form of the human condition, nor is there any support for thinking that it ever will be. To be human is to hear and to use words. And if any of us comes to believe otherwise, it will be because someone's words have misled him into accepting such an unrealistic and irrational conclusion.

[11] *To a Dancing God* (New York: Harper & Row, 1970), pp. 159, 160.

If Keen is sincere in his view that contemporary, post-Reformation man is sick of being inundated in an ocean of verbiage, it is odd that he should appear so willing to add more water to this ocean. Of course, he really has no choice if he wishes to persuade others to share his opinions. You can belittle the use of words only by using words. It should be said that Keen is not absolutely set against all use of words. His contention that the "time for words" has departed with the arrival of the present actually means that the time for relying wholly on words has gone. If we know what is good for us, the sacred *must* be rediscovered in what moves and touches us; the "word" *must* be rediscovered in the flesh; and religion *must* return to dance.

Keen's triple "must," however, indicates a dogmatic stance; and, by his own admission, doctrines belong to the time for words. Thus the inconsistency of his position remains. The remedy for verbiage, surely, ought to lie in a better use of words, not in the hope that we shall return to preverbal consciousness. The desire to reverse history and find a way back to "the primal, the primitive, the carnal" is an understandable reaction to the claim of the Christian secularists, who declare contemporary man to have broken free from bondage to the past and to be totally incapable of any experience of the sacred. Yet, like so many reactions, it goes from one extreme to the other. It exchanges a dogmatism of progress for a dogmatism of primitivism. Actually, we do not know with any certainty what the primitive imagination was like. What we do know is that the wish to return to an imagined primitive consciousness freer and healthier than one's own is a frequent phenomenon in sophisticated societies. This particular wish has a long historical pedigree and is found conspicuously in the Romantic tradition.

In spite of his criticisms of Romanticism, it seems clear that Keen belongs to this tradition. Like Rousseau, he believes that primitive man was a child of nature. Adding the mandatory catchword "radical," Keen speaks of "the universal human birthright of radical freedom."[12] At the same time, he blames the "gnostic" element in Christianity for its failure "to discern the sacred in the voice of the body." Again, Keen fails to recognize the tradition in which he stands. For the Gnostics did not deny this manifestation of the sacred. They affirmed it. What they denied was the reality of the individual body-bounded ego. Accepting immersion in carnal life — especially in the sex act — was always one of their favored ways for liberating the spirit of man from bondage to the illusion of individual existence and for revealing the sacred as an immediate experience. Also, for the Romantic heirs to the gnostic vision, the body was (like nature itself, of which it was the expression) the prime locus of the sacred.

It is an axiom of the Romantic tradition that no genuine experience can be described in words. That is why, for instance, Walter Pater said that all art constantly aspires towards the condition of music. For the Romantic imagination, music is pure sensation and immediate as words never can be. To anyone familiar with the Romantic tradition, then, Keen's statement that the age of hearing is gone and the sacred must be discovered in what moves and touches us is no novel doctrine. In its wider manifestation, of course, the Romantic tradition goes back to the Dionysian dance itself. The ecstasy of the dance extinguishes the individual consciousness, making either speaking or hearing unnecessary. As Yeats wrote, "How can we know the dancer from the dance?"

Although Keen draws back from the logic of his premises, the belittling of the role of speech and the demand that religion return to the dance can only result in the abolition of meaning from individual existence. Moreover, an ideal of radical freedom is incompatible with the acknowledgment of real relationships with others. For if we are to recognize the reality and relative independence of other persons, we have to be ready to do more than

[12]*Ibid.*, p. 136. "No saviors are necessary to confer this freedom." And Keen proceeds to give the usual denunciation of the "Magical" idea of atonement traditional among both the Romantics and the champions of Enlightenment.

invite them to be moved or touched and to join with them in a Dionysian dance. We have to speak to them and hear them speaking to us.

Using and trusting words does not mean that in our bodily existence we have no other means of expression except the verbal or that nonverbal forms of communication are unimportant. But it does mean recognizing that words are both the most important and the most *personal* means of human communication. Bereft of speech and hearing we are left in a world shorn of all true human meaning. And those who would persuade us that direct experience is incompatible with speech ask us to deprive ourselves of our true heritage as human beings. In particular, they demand that our experience of the sacred be wholly impersonal.

Christian faith uses words. It trusts in the adequacy of words to be more than verbiage and to mediate the real to us. Through the words of the gospel we hear the divine Other address us as individuals. We are assured that we are real beings in communication with "him who is real." Christian faith is — and always has to be — the hearing of the word of the living God. Supremely, too, that word is heard in the incarnate Word, Jesus Christ. As the Word, Jesus Christ is the completely personal revelation of the living God, not only because he uses words that address us, but chiefly because he *is* the communicating Word in his own person. Believers do not simply have faith in the truths he uttered during his earthly life. They have faith in him as an individual person. "I am the way; I am the truth; and I am life; no one comes to the Father except by me" (John 14:6).

An idolatrous belief in radical freedom — a freedom, apparently, to be reached by a servile acceptance of a battery of *musts* — results in rendering whole areas of human experience meaningless. The god promising radical freedom takes away our individual existence as persons and demands that we neither speak nor hear. Once we are assured that the time for words is gone, we may be the more easily persuaded that life is really death and that "sacred necessity" is true freedom. But faith in the living God invites us to find meaning and truth in words and to choose intelligently between life and death instead of accepting doctrinaire *musts*. So it is said in the Old Testament: "Today I offer you the choice of life and good, or death and evil" (Deut. 30:15). And the New Testament tells us that our joy may be complete, for "our theme is the word of life" (I John 1:1).

8

THE REALISM OF WORSHIP

Intimations of the Real

So far I have been concentrating on the baleful effects of idolatry and on the need for us to discredit popular myths if we are to escape losing touch with reality. The biblical call is — for us today as much as it was for first-century Christians — to turn from idolatrous follies to the living God. But there is another side to the picture. Idols are shams, but they are shams that exercise power over men's imaginations. The dynamics of the nonexistent is real enough, in that it drives us to definite action in the world, even though this action leads to chaos and destruction. No idol could tempt us to worship it if it did not represent, in a confused and distorted form, some real and positive value. While idolatry leads us away from the truth into deceiving myths, it draws its hazy inspiration from some aspect of created reality, which it then proceeds to develop one-sidedly.

In an essay entitled "The Funeral of a Great Myth"[1] C. S. Lewis once took a shrewd look at the belief in inevitable progress. Although it is usually linked with the scientific attitude, this belief has been made imaginatively persuasive by artists like Keats and Wagner. Lewis insists

[1] In *Christian Reflections* by C. S. Lewis, edited by Walter Hooper (Grand Rapids: Eerdmans, 1967), pp. 82-93.

that "it is imagination which makes the Myth." He details
how contradictory and unreal many of the elements consti-
tuting the Myth of Progress are, and how the Myth's
attractiveness depends on luring us into a dream world.
Were we to keep our eyes on the facts, Lewis suggests,
we should see at once that any given change in society is at
least as likely to destroy the liberties and amenities we
already have as it is to add new ones; and that a prudent
society must spend at least as much on conserving what it
has as it does on improvement. (This was written before
"conservation" became a household word!) If the Myth
survives, Lewis adds, it will be because it continues successfully to obscure knowledge of our actual situation, for

> *It has great allies,*
> *Its friends are propaganda, party cries,*
> *And bilge, and Man's incorrigible mind.*

Nevertheless, it has other and better allies also:

> It appeals to the same innocent and permanent need in us that
> welcomes Jack the Giant Killer. It gives us almost everything
> the imagination craves — irony, heroism, vastness, unity in
> multiplicity, and a tragic close. It appeals to every part of me
> except my reason.[2]

Lewis's funeral oration on the Myth of Progress was
premature. The Myth is still very much around; indeed, it
has gotten a new lease of life by gaining from the romantic
imagination the support that it was beginning to lose from
the scientific-humanistic imagination. Yet the analysis of the
Myth that Lewis makes in his essay is as pertinent today
as it was when he wrote it. In addition, the lesson he draws
from his survey of this particular Myth is true of all myths.

The positive function of myth is to stimulate our imaginations and to promote intelligent thinking by giving us
images to express our thoughts.[3] Myths are the indispensable
seedbeds for growing the images that nourish the imagina-

[2]*Ibid.*, p. 93.

[3]In *Words and the Word*, especially Chapter 2, "Myths, Mythic Patterns,
and History," this is described at greater length.

tion and promote the development of language. They mislead only when we mistake them for historical events, and *vice versa*. Then it happens that men are drawn down the path of idolatry. Instead of nourishing our imaginations, superstitiously venerated myths poison them; and, as I have argued, we find the phenomenon of the atrophy of the imagination evidenced by a supine reliance on stock responses that supplant an imaginative perception of reality. Yet, even in its decay, the power of imaginative thinking to stimulate and inspire us is never wholly lost.

Thus we should heed C. S. Lewis's reminder that idolatrous myths have a good side as well as a thoroughly bad side. Such myths deceive the mind, enticing us away from reality into a Never-Never Land of appealing dreams. In encouraging us to seek reality in dreams, they may cause us to have nightmares and to waken in a mood of frightened and irrational despair. Yet we need to be able to dream, to have visions, and to be inspired by ideals as yet unrealized. Dream-life and waking-life are each a part of the human condition, and there is a place for both in our human experience. Our mental health is endangered only when we lose the ability to distinguish the one from the other.

In every myth there is an intimation of the real. The fact that no tribe or nation on earth is without its myths of the gods witnesses to the truth that mankind has been created to worship the Creator. The continual rise of idolatries in every age points to a deadly sickness affecting the imagination of men's hearts. Yet it also points to the fact that those restless hearts that can find their rest in the living God alone are perpetually searching for some divinity to worship. The unreal images of idol-worshipers contain some flickering image of the God who is real. Whenever men elevate one created power or another to the status of a divinity, their distorted imaginations still are turned to something that has a measure of reality — though not the reality imagined. Even rebellious powers unwillingly serve divine providence.

Turning away from idols, then, is not simply a matter of

ignoring them. Paul warned the Christians at Corinth that
saying an idol is nothing is insufficient. Such so-called
knowledge does not edify; it does not build up the community of faith; it is deficient in love for the brethren. In the
terminology that I have been using, it might be said that
the deficiency in love displayed by self-assured knowledge
is a deficiency in the imagination. For example, it fails to
consider the imaginative outlook of the brother whose
conscience is weak. Love always reaches out to the other
— to God and to our neighbor. And without imaginative
sympathy love is impossible. We can love our neighbor as
ourselves only by imagining ourselves in his place, and thus
seeing the world through his eyes. Moreover, self-assured
knowledge assumes that it already knows the entire truth.
It lacks humility before the truth, and so it also lacks the
self-knowledge necessary for humble service of the truth.

The idolatrous beliefs we surveyed in Part Two have
lessons to teach us because all of them exhibit intimations
of the real. If they did not, the idol could not wear the
mask of the one true God and tempt us to worship it.
The cult of relevance reminds us that we live in time. The
past — although we can never afford to ignore it without
making ourselves cosmic orphans — is not the place where
we can live. We are not our fathers, and we cannot live
in their world. The gospel is true for all times, but we can
know its truth only when we find it to be true for ours. The
worship of the Great God Change reminds us that nothing
stands still in the world, and that we must always move to
progress or to regress. Fear of the new and nostalgia for
the old is, finally, despair of the created order and unwilling-
ness to trust the Lord, who makes all things new (Rev. 21:5).
Looking to the promised land of liberation, equally, is a
summons to our spirits to follow the living God who leads
us through the desert to the New Jerusalem.

What we have to discover is a way of keeping the vision
that appears in a distorted form through the myths cherished
by current idolatries, while cutting loose from the net of
unreal dreams into which these idolatries attempt to lure us.
In order to keep our minds clear and focused on the real

instead of on deceiving and confusing myths (II Tim. 4:4), we shall have to understand the gospel through the full exercise of our imaginations. Stock responses, even if they are responses to revealed truth and hallowed by traditional usage, are never enough. If we can keep our imaginations supple and responsive, we can hear God's word speaking to the particular needs of our generation as well as to the needs of all generations. After all, it matters much less that the word should be thought "believable" than that the word should accomplish the purpose of the living God (Isa. 55:11) through us rather than in spite of us. It may be a lie that traditional language about faith is "not living" and incomprehensible to contemporary man. Nevertheless, some ways of speaking about (and thinking about) faith may be more alive and more comprehensible than others; and it is the duty of contemporary Christians to find out what these ways are.

Awakening from the Dream of Secular Man

The cult of relevance, resting consciously or unconsciously on the dogma of the Perennial New, assumes that the historical continuity that links each generation to the next can be ignored, and that contemporary man is fated only to be able to understand the contemporary form of the revealed word of the Great God Change.

This assumption, of course, makes nonsense of history. It confuses the abstraction "contemporary man" with actual people now living, who carry in their imaginations all sorts of images learned from the traditions in which they have been raised. Since men tend to transform reality into the images of their dreams, however, communication between people actually has become more difficult. Alienation — that invention of the Hegelian philosophy — obsesses men's mind. As the Self images the Other as an enemy, individuals find that they cannot relate themselves within an ordered community to other individuals. The abstract bogey of the identity crisis gives them dismay. The generation gap is erected into a wall on which the guns of confrontation are poised. All this comes from believing that there can be no imaginative understanding between one age and the next.

Yet, in the real world, human consciousness is one consciousness. It has been the same so far as we have any record of it. The evidence of this is given in its unique product — art. The cave drawings of prehistoric man, early Chinese bronzes, Egyptian wall-paintings, Greek sculpture, Byzantine icons, Medieval carvings, Renaissance frescos, Dutch still-life and landscape paintings, Rococo plaster-word and porcelain, Victorian steel-engravings, modern op-pop-and-dynamic art — all show us a bewildering number of styles and a single sensibility. Art in any period may be inspired by art from any other period. Artists go back to the past in order to see their way through to a "truly contemporary" style.

Literature teaches this lesson even more clearly. The earliest writings of man speaking about himself and his world are as immediately comprehensible to us as are the latest. The Song of Deborah echoes in modern ears with as much power, and reflects the human spirit as fully, as does a song by Leonard Cohen. (A recent popular folk song, indeed, was simply a transcript of some verses of Ecclesiastes!) Sophocles, Dante, and Wordsworth speak as understandably to contemporary men as do Allen Ginsberg, Norman Mailer, and Lawrence Ferlinghetti. Only a blind and stupid dogmatism would dispute this, or argue that the past means nothing to us today and the contemporary consciousness is a wholly new thing in a wholly new world.

For some time, we have been told that the wholly new man is the man with a radically secular consciousness. During the sixties and into the seventies scores of books issuing from the religious presses have argued that only a radically secular faith could hope to inherit the future. The recent course of actual events, of course, has made this claim slightly unbelievable. The following fictionalized dialogue may illustrate what I mean.

Theologian A. I had an interesting time addressing an open-air meeting sponsored by The Society for a Relevant Secular Christianity.

Theologian B. You spoke, of course, about how a truly contemporary person cannot be religious.

A. Yes. I explained that not only is God-talk meaningless today, but that the modern mind is totally incapable of grasping every form of transcendence. Even religion without God, I argued (laboring the obvious), is only a halfway position still influenced by the ghost of traditional Christianity. The really revolutionary stance enthrones secular man as the sole responsible arbiter of the cosmos.

B. You had an enthusiastic response?

A. Well, actually, a Maoist speaker next to me rather drowned me out. But I didn't mind, for he shows the form that genuine secularity is taking in our age.

B. That certainly shows how undogmatic Christian secularity is, and how open to the future.

A. Getting down from the platform I had to elbow aside an astrologer, a warlock and a covey of witches, a swami, a man with Tarot cards, another with I Ching, a bunch of Krishna devotees, several Jesus people, and some assorted Jehovah's Witnesses, Mormons, Roman Catholic Pentecostals, Baptists, and a man who gave me a pamphlet about the Great Pyramid. But it was Thursday, and Thursday is my lucky day. I wasn't hurt.

B. Thank God for that. I must be off now. I have to baby-sit while my wife goes off to her cell-group — one of those speaking-with-tongues affairs. I don't approve of it, naturally. But it gives me time for my transcendental meditation.

A. I don't believe in that, either. But then I'm a Scorpio. We Scorpios are highly skeptical.

There is nothing very surprising about the evident turning away from the secularistic mentality now going on around us. Human consciousness has always known a three-story universe. When men are told that they must accept the horizontal, earthbound consciousness as the only one that really exists, sooner or later they will rebel against a theory contradicting the images latent in their imaginations. To find

their way back to a world-view that includes the vertical
line of the supernatural above and below middle-earth,
they will welcome any system of belief that admits the
three-story universe. Because, indeed, it is *modern* science
that is blamed for taking away man's former vision, the
more archaic and superstitious the world-view happens to
be, the more attractive it will seem.

Since Christianity appears to have capitulated to the
scientific outlook, it is suspect to the rebels against secular-
ism. Some, though, accept a Christian faith of a simple,
charismatic type that can claim to be Christianity as it
originally was before it was assimilated to a thisworldly and
sophisticated culture. Others simply bypass the Christian
tradition altogether, thinking they can find an older (and
thus purer) truth in Oriental mysticism. Still others go back
to the oldest of all springs of religious consciousness, the
stars, the ageless rulers of the sky that watch and guide the
actions of men beneath them; or to the white and black
magical powers that descend from heaven and rise out of
hell to possess the human soul stationed on middle-earth.

In short, the secularized consciousness is an empty house.
Swept and garnished, it welcomes the arrival of spirits good
or evil. Even after being educated by scientific humanists
and by secularizing theologians in the belief that contemporary man has come of age and needs no gods, contemporary
men are dimly aware that they have been deprived of an
essential part of their humanity. Their imaginative selves
cry out for something to worship directly and visibly.

Of course, secular Christianity was never actually a
godless creed. It was an idolatry turning to its own god, the
Great God Change, and to the transcendence that it
imagined was embodied in the work of the god, who was
then identified with the biblical God retiring (in Hegelian
fashion) and handing over his power to secular man.[4] That
was why its exponents, after denying the possibility of any
specifically religious expression of transcendence in contemporary life, could so easily go on to affirm the religious

4See *What's New in Religion?*, especially Part 2, "About the New Themes,"
and Part 4, "About the Secular in Faith and Morals."

quality of life itself as a cause for celebration.[5] It meant only
a little change in emphasis, one that swung away from the
mechanistic image of external progress and doxologies to
technopolitan man's great creation; and swung instead
towards the organic image of the life force and hymned
the praises of the inner divine spirit in man's own immediate consciousness. Having previously admired most
the Hegelians of the Left, they now are prepared to speak
like Hegelians of the Right.

Yet most of the secularizing theologians, though
emboldened by the running tide of the return to believing
and worshiping, have been afraid to move too fast or too far.
Committed to the dogma that the form of the Perennial
New dictates faith which we *must* follow as our fate, they
are prepared to admit the legitimacy of formerly scorned
religious ritual. They will even flirt with the god Dionysus,
though they are not quite prepared to confess his full
divinity. They are still convinced, however, that contemporary man is too sophisticated to believe that there can
be actual gods and devils. The abstract contemporary man
of their imagination has insulated them against contact with
real contemporary individuals who have no such inhibitions
and who are tired of feeding on the meager religious crumbs
that fall from the secularists' tables.

We are witnessing in the rise of extravagant religious
cults a movement away from the abstract monotheism that
has dominated Western thought since the rise of scientific
humanism. That monotheism has become intolerably anti-
septic and forbidding since theologians began to ridicule
the idea that contemporary man could believe in a personal
God "out there." Better magic and superstition than iron
law, even though it be labeled the creating-destroying
process. Awakening from the dream of radically secular
man, men have found themselves as hungry for religion as
ever. And they demand real religions, with gods and shrines
and sacrifices, not some pale, abstract, sophisticated
substitute.

[5]As Harvey Cox did when he followed up *The Secular City* (1965) by
The Feast of Fools (Cambridge: Harvard U.P., 1970).

Worship as Celebration

Through the cracks in the walls of the Secular City, then, we are once more hearing the sounds of worship — real honest-to-goodness worship with public prayers, hymns, creeds, and sacramental acts.

When men actually worship a god, even an idol, they recognize an Other to whom they are related in community. Worship in the mind alone will not achieve this, especially if the object of worship is abstract and ideological and the place of creeds is taken by slogans and catchwords. But in acting out the rituals of worship men find themselves brought into harmony with their fellows and with the environing world. There is no doubt why mass rallies are so important in totalitarian countries. The indoctrination of individuals by schooling them in the collective dogmas is not enough. There has to be a ritual public enactment of the solidarity of a whole people united not only under their rulers but also with them "in spirit."

Today we all realize how far we shall have to travel if we are to discover any kind of unified world in an age oppressed by a sense of alienation and full of partisan factions, each engaged in issuing nonnegotiable demands for liberation *now*. When theologians cry that what we need is revolutionary action, the divisive situation is only aggravated. Making revolution into a catchword supposed (by stock response) to be the solution for everything merely adds to the existing confusion. It does not help us to distinguish social and political conditions in which revolution may be the only answer from the mass of other conditions in which revolution is not only undesirable but also impossible and absurd. It might be genuinely revolutionary if theologians were to urge us to undertake the discipline of worship. While such a recommendation would certainly raise the stock response of "Escapism!" it would be a word of actual realism.

The realism of worship is A. G. Hebert's theme in his

eminently sane book *Liturgy and Society*.[6] Father Hebert
(a "High Church" Anglican, incidentally) wrote nearly forty
years ago; yet, even then, in times much less obviously
apocalyptic than ours, he noted the disintegration of modern
life, the confusion of belief, and "the falling in ruins of the
towers of Babel that human idealism tries to build." He
writes of his conviction that worship, expressed through
the church's liturgy, can bring a sense of unity into a world
that, as it grows ever more crowded and mechanized, is
burdened with an increasing sense of fragmentation and
meaninglessness. But he insists — and this seems to me to be
crucial — that the sense of unity given through participation
in worship can never be sought as an end in itself. The
foundation of worship is, as he terms it, *ontological* and not
psychological. That is, worship undertaken because we want
to feel a sense of support and "belonging" is self-defeating.
Worship is good for us, Hebert argues, because it speaks to
us "of a real relation of man to the Eternal."

Undoubtedly, the hope that they will gain a sense of being
in a real relation to what is permanent and sure has drawn
many to seek in worship what they cannot find in the
ideological worship of the Great God Change. For that god
does not enter into any actual relationship with his worshipers; instead, he demands passive submission to his
abstract laws of progress-through-process. Like Esau many
today feel that they have been cheated out of their birthright
in exchange for a mess of secular pottage. Like Esau they
are left crying with a great and exceedingly bitter cry,
"Bless me, even me also, O my father." Is it already too
late to expect such a blessing?

In the climate of present-day culture, worship is more
often a problem than a blessing. The sense of community
is so weak and impoverished that people rarely find relationships giving healing and support except in small groups
where everyone can know everyone else quite intimately.
Indeed, ours is a day of groups: neighborhood groups, cell
groups, sensitivity groups, Esalen groups, activity groups,

[6]*Liturgy and Society: The Function of the Church in the Modern World*
(London: Faber & Faber, 1935).

meditation groups, and cult groups. Traditional worship
has nearly always been designed for a larger congregation
than the group-meeting. It has envisaged a gathering-in of a
whole community, or at least of a representative portion
thereof. In the traditional churches the comprehensive
congregation is still considered normative. This means that
church worship is a problem. It does not give us the support
of intimacy that we associate with "real" community.
Complaints about the coldness, formality, and impersonality
of ordinary worship services are widespread.

One popular response to these complaints is typified by
the current catchword "celebration." The choice of the
word, I fancy, comes from an effort to dissociate public
worship from the stock image of church services. Churches,
as everyone knows, are dull places where dull congregations
go through dull routine. So break away! Don't worship —
celebrate. Don't quench the Spirit — liberate it. Up go
colored posters with bright slogans announcing that "Christ
was the First Revolutionary" and the like, and the outlines
of traditional architecture are consequently masked. In come
the rock groups (yes, *groups*). Members of the congregation
are given buttons displaying their first names. They are encouraged to introduce themselves all round, shake hands,
give the kiss of peace, and even to join in a liturgy containing
a (rather subdued) Dionysian dance.

Insofar as the word "celebration" and its accompanying
revamping of the liturgy gives a better public image of
worship and what it is all about, it is really useful. That is,
it is useful psychologically. I am not so happy about what
it assumes ontologically speaking, which is to say, about
what the people who urge us to forget our middle-class
inhibitions and celebrate with spontaneous joy actually
imagine celebration to be.

"Celebration" is a noble word, and I would be the last
to belittle it. A dictionary definition is: "To perform the
ceremony of, in a public and solemn manner." The celebrationists are right, I am sure, in reminding us that "solemn" need not mean dull. The passive and lethargic
congregational attitude seen in many Christian churches

in this century is positively un-Christian, if Christianity is in truth a faith that gives freedom and joy. On the other hand, I am personally not at all convinced that the proper way of countering the bad tradition of congregational passivity is to try to whip up a spirit of camaraderie quite suitable for an intimate group but quite artificial in the context of a larger and differently constituted assembly. Buttonholing familiarity and the extra-friendly handshake marked a species of pietism born some time in the last century. Many would be glad to see this parody of Christian fellowship safely buried once and for all.

If celebration is to be understood in the sense of "performing the ceremony of," that little word "of" becomes all-important. Very easily, celebration takes on the much narrower sense that it has borrowed from our culture. Instead of standing for a ceremonial representation of a specific belief about man's relation to the Eternal, it can stand for little more than our wish to feel stimulated by throwing a party. (The book-jacket of Harvey Cox's *The Feast of Fools,* for example, shows the author and his family wearing funny hats and having a picnic in what seems to be their backyard.) Especially when former advocates of secular Christianity turn into celebrationists, I sense a change of mood rather than a change of heart and imagination. Even putting up a handwritten sign in the sanctuary proclaiming "Christ Is Risen" does not necessarily mean that our celebration is of his resurrection rather than of our own attempts to resurrect feelings of well-being and *ersatz* brotherly love.

Worship as Response to the Real

"Celebration of life" is the stock phrase supposed to be a sufficient answer to the question of why we should see worship as celebration. But if the life we are urged to celebrate is an ecstasy of mere vitalism, we shall sooner or later have to stop playing with words, clear our heads, and face plain facts. Celebrating life by joining in the Dionysian dance gives us at best a drunken euphoria tonight that has to be paid for by a hangover tomorrow morning. Continuing in the dance leads to madness and self-destruction. For to hope for fulness of life on this level is to embrace a "sickness unto death" born of despair.[7] In the end our celebration of life will be to gaze into the impersonal eyes of the Great God Change and acknowledge his implacable immutability.

Imagining that life is found on the organic level alone is part of what the New Testament means when it speaks of the natural man and of living according to the flesh.[8] The "fleshly man" (Col. 2:18 KJV) is precisely the man whose imagination creates some religion that satisfies his needs — as he conceives them to be. But in the process he loses hold upon "the solid reality" which "is Christ's" (Col. 2:17 NEB). The Scriptures connect life according to the flesh with the inability of men to look realistically at the laws by which the living God orders his world and with their rejection of his Word sent for their salvation. Paul writes in Romans:

> To set the mind on the flesh is death, but to set the mind on the Spirit is life and peace. For the mind that is set on the flesh is hostile to God; it does not submit to God's law, indeed it cannot; and those who are in the flesh cannot please God (Rom. 8:6-8 RSV).

When life is understood as more than a plunge into the abyss of the life force, when it is accepted as personal life lived in relation to the Creator and Redeemer, physical death is no longer cause for despair. Death remains man's "last

---

[7] Søren Kierkegaard analyzed the forms of this kind of despair, ranging them between the seemingly complacent and the seemingly heroic. See *The Sickness Unto Death* in *Fear and Trembling and The Sickness Unto Death* (Garden City, N.Y.: Doubleday, 1954), pp. 162-207.

[8] Trying to find words that fit into the twentieth-century vocabulary better than "flesh" and "fleshly" (for *sarx* and *sarkikos*), modern translators run into difficulties. Such choices as "unspiritual" or "on the level of our lower nature" or "by worldly standards" are more misleading than helpful. There is really no simple way of explaining the biblical image of the created world as the world of *flesh*, a world that is good in itself but that becomes "a body of death" when it does not see itself in relation to the living God, its Creator and Redeemer.

enemy" still, but it is no longer something that we must accept because the destroying-creating process demands it for its own continued life. The death of the man Jesus Christ has given us freedom to mock the power of death (I Cor. 15:55), because we are now assured that it is subject to the power of the Most High since it has been defeated by the resurrection in history of the Son of God.

Thus, what our worship is celebration *of* is the remembrance of what God has actually done for us. The ceremonies of worship center in this corporate memory. Because it includes both Good Friday and Easter, the celebration is solemn as well as joyous. No easy stock response by the worshipers' undisciplined imagination will suffice to provide an image for the Christian memory, which abounds in paradox and mystery.

Moreover, while Christ crucified and resurrected is always at the core of the Christian memory, these central real events give the perspective in which the worshiping community can see all events, both past and present. Worship reflects the totality of human existence and human experience. When we join in worship we relate the whole of life to the knowledge and the service of the living God. This means that we cannot bring to worship just our personal experiences (or what we like to imagine as being our experiences) but everything that comes to us from the hand of God.

Forms of worship, therefore, while important are always secondary. It is the total recognition of the relation of our lives to our Creator and Redeemer that keeps worship a living act. Because the fear of death is the great obstacle to our living freely and joyously, this particular fear cannot be swept under the carpet of our subconscious mind or kept at arm's length by the unrealistic thought, "Death isn't so terrible after all, since it's really part of life." To know that life is the living God's will for us, we need to hold on to the memory of the Son who laid down his life in obedience to the Father. The images of our imagination must conform to the solid reality that is Christ's, allowing us to consent to our true relation to the Eternal. "You died; and now your life lies hidden with Christ in God. When Christ, who is our life, is manifested, then you too will be manifested with him in glory" (Col. 3:3-4). Going down into death and rising again through the Father's power — these are the images in which Christian worship expresses itself, images that can be both metaphorical and actual as the situation of our lives happens to require.

So long as our worship is realistic, always pointing to the reality of God's salvation and the reality of the faith to which we as Christian believers have been called, I believe the appropriate forms of it will not be impossible to find. Within the Christian churches, both in those who place high value upon a set liturgy and in those called (mistakenly, I think) nonliturgical, there are traditions to guide us. Adapting those traditions to the present moment should not be too hard. Like everything worth doing, of course, it requires devoted work, strenuous thinking, sensitive imaginations; and it will never be as perfect as we should like. If a great deal of "experimental" worship is soon dated and quickly forgotten, no great harm is done. Only if we continue to think in terms proper only to the worshipers of the Great God Change will our expectations be so high that disillusionment is bound to follow.

Worship cannot always be an intense psychological experience. Sometimes it will be merely routine, so far as our reactions go; sometimes even boring. But that is true of anything that belongs to real life. Only romantics expect always to live at a fever pitch of joyous rapture. Nor should worship ever be considered as a kind of charging of our spiritual batteries, so they can run at high power for the next week. This mistake is encouraged by an inane practice in many churches, which print at the foot of the order of worship, "The worship is ended, the service of God has begun." Worship is part of our living, not an interlude when we take a rest from life.

In worship, indeed, we ought to be more intensely alive than at other times, for it is in worship that we remember what we too often forget at other times. As part of a congregation that is more than a group of people whom we have chosen to meet with because they "understand" us, we are reminded that our lives are not lonely efforts, since they are always related to the Eternal God; and that we do not carry the world's weight on our shoulders, since we are part of the Body of Christ — a Body that did not begin with us and will not end with us. We choose our friends, but we do not choose our fellow-worshipers. God has chosen them for us, as Jesus chose his disciples and then made them his friends (John 15:15-16). We do not choose our place in the Christian tradition, any more than we choose our parents or the date of our birth.

The world around us seems to consider all limitations proof that one is in an alienated state from which liberation must be sought at all costs. But not wishing to be liberated from our service here and now is our "revolutionary" claim as Christian worshipers. No doubt there are those who would consider this hopelessly supine and proof that Christianity is the religion of slaves. But who needs to be liberated when he is already free? Jesus said, "In the world you will have trouble. But courage! The victory is mine; I have conquered the world" (John 16:33).

For those with a poor quality imagination, sitting in a service of worship may seem an odd place from which to proclaim the victory of freedom. But no one suggests that Christians (other than in exceptional circumstances) are going to spend their whole life there. Dietrich Bonhoeffer believed that the modern Christian's place was in the world, while he nourished his Christian spirit with a "secret Discipline." None understood better than Bonhoeffer that we only know the "secular" world when we see it from the perspective of reality given in worship, and out of a knowledge of Christ's victory over the world. From their different situations Christians balance worship and secular activity in different proportions. But no Christian who values the tradition in which he stands can doubt that the nonworshiping world does not know either the secular or the sacred life as the worshiper comes to know it. Nowhere else than in worship are we related to the solid reality that is Christ's Lordship over the world.

Images in Worship

Worship is psychologically mediated, and there are
psychological factors in contemporary life that make it hard
for us to open ourselves to the reality of worship. One is
that worship is ceremonious, and everyday life today is
destructive of ceremony in general. Incessant propaganda
decries traditions of every kind and apparently is blandly
ignorant of the human purpose of ceremonial behavior.

I would add in passing that the almost universal disregard
for ceremony is no small part of the reason why violence
is multiplying around us. For civilization and ceremony
are almost synonymous terms; and contempt for ceremony
is the most certain way of guaranteeing a regression into
barbarism. It is perhaps significant that the people most
punctilious about ceremonies at present are the Satanists
and witches. At least when they are performing their religious rites, they would rather die than deviate a hair's
breadth from the prescribed rituals; indeed, they usually
believe that death would follow any such deviation. But
then they are proud of their traditions, which, as they like
to boast, are much older than Christianity and go back to
the beginnings of civilization.

Another psychological factor that makes worship seem
strange to us is the result of our progressivist dogmas. The
automobile image is still potent in influencing our imaginative attitude to the world. Because we tend to resent anything
that is not immediately useful for controlling our environment, we do not perceive and draw comfort from the
structures of nature that are analogous to our own human
structures, or from her rhythms that correspond with ours.
Yet, without such a perception, the symbols that make up
the ceremonies of worship cannot be understood. We
expect that worship should be immediately useful, that it
should visibly increase our vitality and efficiency when we
leave the "unreality" of the sanctuary and enter what we
take to be real life — the activities of the Secular City and
the scramble to achieve liberation by "keeping pace."

It might be thought that the present emphasis on organic

process would reverse this activist-progressivist trend. Unfortunately it has done nothing of the sort. Because the vision of life as a process has incorporated into itself the mechanistic-progressive dogma, it remains abstract. Romantically in love with the process for its own sake, it ignores the real and living face of created nature. In this connection we have only to remember how the word "structures" has become a dirty word along with "tradition." Structures are regarded as barriers that have to be overthrown in order to achieve liberation. It is conveniently forgotten that both the body of nature and fabric of human society are made up of interrelated structures, structures developed through history and coexisting through a delicate balance of their constituent parts.

Worship cannot exist without structures. These structures may be tightly organized, as they are in formal liturgical worship, or loosely organized, as they are in so-called nonliturgical worship; but if they are not there, worship will soon degenerate into something else — an exercise in self-expression by the leader, a session for indoctrination in current ideologies, a time of psychological conditioning in "progressive" or "reactionary" cultural attitudes, or an opportunity for indulging in mass hysteria. Structures of worship are inherited from tradition; though, as always happens in a living tradition, they develop and change while preserving continuity with the past. The elements of worship are ceremonies or ritual actions within a structure: prayer, praise, reading of the Scriptures, sermon, sacramental acts, and so on. These elements are themselves structured, and the building blocks of the elements of worship are symbols or images.

Without images, for example, we could not hear the Scriptures when they are read in worship. (Hearing is itself a biblical image, of course, signifying understanding in obedience instead of merely listening to the words.) Hardly a phrase of the Bible reaches our ears without presenting a lively image for our imaginations to receive: *the Lord is my strength and song; rise up, O Lord; the Lord is my shepherd; Ho, every one that thirsteth; as the rain cometh down;*

turn you to the stronghold, ye prisoners of hope; the field is the world; I am the bread of life; for thy sake we are killed all the day long; our God is a consuming fire; behold, I come as a thief; I am the root and offspring of David, and the bright and morning star. However familiar these images may become, none of them invites a stock response. Individually, each directs us to turn to the real world of the Creator and, through the aid of his works, to hear his word. Also, because one image reinforces another, we become aware of how Scripture is the interpreter of Scripture. We are not permitted so to dwell with one image alone that we construct an idol out of it, resting in the Creator's works instead of in the Eternal himself.

The danger of using any image is always that we are tempted to stay with it as a sufficient revelation of truth, and no imaginative picture of anything in heaven or on earth can be this. The celebrationists, for instance, urge us to celebrate life under the image of a feast. But life is not just a feast. It is true that a feast is right at the heart of Christian worship. As a well-loved Communion hymn tells us:

> *This is the hour of banquet and of song;*
> *This is the heavenly table spread for me;*
> *Here let me feast. . . .*

In order to make feasting an act of worship, we must be willing to make an offering of fasting too. Dietrich Bonhoeffer reminds us that no Christian can expect the new day of Easter resurrection unless he is first willing to watch with Christ at Gethsemane.

Harvey Cox urges us to celebrate a Feast of Fools. Yet, in order to recognize the truth about this particular celebration, we have to remember its context. Setting up a Lord of Misrule (in order to recall the fact that God chooses the foolish to confound the wise) was a ceremony meaningful in medieval society. There obedience was normally given unquestioningly to authorities who were recognized to be wise and prudent. The Feast of Fools was one of those exceptions which find their significance in the rule to which they are the exception. We cannot today revive the exception while ignoring the rule. If we try to do so, we shall have nothing to celebrate. All images are like that. One-sidedly developed, they lead us away from reality. They dupe us into believing that we can make our world to the model of any image that we happen to fancy, whereas the truth is that we shall destroy ourselves unless we keep our images true to the wholeness of life as it comes to us from its Maker.

In worship we are continually brought back from the misuse of images. Today the image of youthfulness is constantly held before us as a realizable ideal provided we eat the right food, buy the right cosmetics, and "think young." In fact, we grow old; and in worship we are reminded constantly of the day when "the evening comes, and the fever of life is over, and our work is done." We want to forget that we must die, and we turn the corpses of our dead into grinning parodies of life. We even insist that funerals should be "cheerful." Yet, just as winter is as much part of our earthly experience as springtime, so sorrow and mourning belong to our lives as well as joyous celebration. We cannot worship the Lord of life unless we also acknowledge that he knows our end and the time of our departing. Worship reminds us, "In the midst of life we are in death." There is a time to be cheerful, but there is also a time to be solemn. "Rejoice always" (Phil. 4:4); yes, but not always with smiles on our faces. The knowledge that God will wipe away all tears from our eyes does not mean that it is never proper to cry. Jesus too wept (John 11:35).

Images used in worship, therefore, are protected from collapsing into stock responses. Instead, they keep our imaginations properly alive and alert. Worship, like life itself, is sometimes routine and at such times we expect little or nothing from it. But, again like life itself, worship is not to be undertaken simply for what we expect to get out of it, or cherished only when it is obviously satisfying and rewarding, Worship is indeed the key to living bravely and in the belief that our Creator knew what he was doing

when he created us, so that dull patches of experience
may at any time break into new unfolding of wonder and
beauty and truth. But worship is not to be entered into,
any more than marriage is, for its psychological rewards.
It is coming into a real relation with the Eternal that
matters.

The solemn ceremonies of worship are, as a matter of
fact, psychologically rewarding. These same ceremonies
bring order and meaning into our lives. In worship our
imaginations are quickened and enlarged through our discovery of how to use rightly the images in worship. Marking
each season of existence with an alternating rhythm of joy
and sorrow, of activity and repose, worship overcomes the
sense of cosmic alienation. It banishes the emptiness that
haunts all human efforts to make life worth living.

But, naturally, it is not the ceremonies in themselves that
accomplish this, needful as they are for the human psyche.
It is the "ontological" significance of the ceremonies that
really heals us. In worship we know with certainty that we
are not passing shadows, but held firm in relation to the
Eternal. The Eternal himself, through his word, gives us
this certainty. Because the living God rules life and death,
none of the aspects of either can be too fearsome to face
directly and realistically. Nothing, neither life nor death,
nor disillusionment over the past, nor future shock, nor the
chaos of the present, nor institutions, nor technological
depersonalization, nor unknown forces within our unconscious — nothing in all creation can sever us from the love
of God made visible in Jesus Christ. Paul, making his own
catalog of enemies of human life, said, "For I am convinced" (Rom. 8:38). Whenever the convincing character
of Christian faith begins to wane in us, we need to find
renewal of our faith in worship. Psychologically, we require
to be refreshed by the reality of the images used in worship.
Ontologically, we require to be brought into the congregation of the faithful so that we may stand before the
living Lord.

9

THE OBEDIENT FREEDOM OF PREACHING

Is Preaching Obsolete?

If all the ceremonies of worship are under attack, the sermon is especially unpopular, because it seems peculiarly irrelevant. The reason for continuing to carry this particular piece of traditional baggage is not readily apparent.

In a rapidly changing world, why is the old practice of preaching retained in an unchanged form? Is the platform speaker not becoming rapidly obsolete in an age of mass communication media? When people are used to specialists in every other field, might not the churches be wise to delegate all preaching and teaching to trained radio and television experts? And, anyway, is not the very idea of one man speaking down from a pulpit to a silent congregation a relic of those days long past when the masses passively accepted what their leaders told them? Would not congregational discussion — or better still, small-group interchange — be more fitting in an era of participatory democracy?

My personal response to such questions is that most of the issues raised are interesting and all of them worth debating. Where techniques of communicating the gospel are concerned, there is indeed a need for understanding and exploiting new forms for spreading around the old message. But preaching in church is not primarily a teaching device. First and foremost, it is a ceremony of the church's worship. In this regard it is not an optional exercise or a practice to be judged by its "usefulness." In addition, preaching today has — or could have — a very important role in bringing home to us what worship is all about, since in the ceremony of the sermon ritual action is combined with a direct address to the congregation by the leader (or one of the leaders) of worship. This unique character of the sermon within the total structure of worship makes it nonexpendable. But, of course, we should have a quite definite understanding of what the role of preaching is in worship, and of how the sermon stands in relation to the rest of the ceremonies of worship. Critics of preaching as it now is practiced are perfectly justified in saying that the sermon should not be retained just because it always has been included on orders of service and people are used to it. No good purpose is ever served by simply going through the motions of an act that has lost all evident meaning.

A case possibly could be made for retaining preaching as part of the Christian church's liturgy, even if it had become quite meaningless in itself. Christianity is an historical religion, and one of the functions of Christian worship is to relate us to Christians of previous generations. So traditional forms should never be changed heedlessly, just because their relevance is no longer obvious. The sermon is so much a part of the Christian tradition that it could not be wholly jettisoned without our losing touch with the Christian past. There is a story (I cannot vouch for its truth) that, when the British Army Manual was revised shortly before World War II, it was discovered that one man in each artillery section was detailed to stand at attention, ten paces apart from his fellows, throughout the action of firing. Through research it was discovered that this was the man who once used to hold the horses that drew the gun carriage. When mechanization came he had to be given something to do, since, though superfluous, he was still there.

But I do not believe that the time has come for the preacher's role to be reduced to that of a token simply providing a link with the past. The figure of a man standing mutely in a pulpit in order to present a liturgical reminder of where the sermon *used* to be suggests pious absurdity rather than solemn memory. No, preaching should be able to justify itself within a living tradition if it is to continue at all. Minor liturgical features of worship may be retained in vestigial form after their original purpose has faded from the corporate memory. But though the importance of the sermon has been variously regarded at different periods in church history, it has never been at the margin of worship. Periods of neglect, however long, have always been followed by periods of vital renewal. Moreover, throughout the whole of church history, from the very beginning, the sermon has provided much of the finest literature that the Christian tradition has produced.

Christian worship is that act in which the congregation recognizes itself as belonging to the fellowship of the Body of Christ, and, under the direction of its head, sanctified in the service of God (I Cor. 12:27; Col. 2:19; Heb. 9:14). The individual ceremonies making up this act of corporate worship are all directed towards re-presenting ("showing forth") the revealed mystery of the Christian gospel, God's saving action for his elect in Jesus Christ, the crucified and risen Son. The eucharist or Lord's supper is the directly symbolic and sacramental rite representing the Christian mystery. "For every time you eat this bread and drink the cup, you proclaim the death of the Lord, until he comes" (I Cor. 11:26). But the mystery is also proclaimed in words recalling the saving action of God as revealed to his people. In the reading of the Scriptures and in the sermon explicating Scripture the worshiping congregation, through its chosen representatives, re-presents the gospel of salvation that came in the Word made flesh.

The justification of the sermon is that it re-presents the human reception of the divine Word. The Word of God accomplishes its purpose by being sown on good soil

(Matt. 13:23), by being heard with obedience (Matt. 7:21). Without the response of man *in his own words,* hearing is incomplete. The words of the preacher supply the genuinely human element in "divine worship."

The Ceremony of Preaching

For Christians standing in the Reformation tradition, the Christian church is defined as being where the word is preached and the sacraments duly administered. Yet, just as the medieval church had emphasized the sacraments at the expense of the word, so the churches of post-Reformation Protestantism have emphasized the preached word at the expense of the sacraments.

In Scotland there are still quite a number of pre-Reformation church buildings of cruciform design. These were erected to provide the best setting for a liturgy of highly developed visual symbolism in which to present the "drama" of the mass. Many of these churches were later cut up into two or three rectangular sanctuaries, because Protestant ministers insisted on having "preaching churches." Protestants objected to the forms of "papist worship," charging that they were full of "frivolous ceremonies" obscuring the direct message of the gospel. The word of God was to be heard, not seen, and worship must be, above all else, the proclamation of the gospel in a way that nothing would prevent its being received by those who had ears to hear.

Sons of the Reformation may believe that these Protestant ministers were right, given the particular historical situation in which they found themselves. Nevertheless, the result was not all gain. The alterations in the church structures were as unfortunate theologically as they were aesthetically. One result was to obscure the fact that the proclamation of Jesus Christ is the revelation of a mystery (Rom. 16:25); and that, in consequence, preaching a sermon is not *in itself* the proclamation of the gospel. The sermon is properly a symbolic act and a ceremony of the church.

If this statement seems surprising, it is because in the Protestant tradition preaching and the message preached — the gospel — have been so frequently equated. This equation, in my opinion, has been the source of real theological confusion. Because two things that should have been carefully distinguished have been telescoped together, the sermon has been put in the wrong category. Many of the current objections to preaching come from an improper identification of preaching with the message preached.

"It pleased God by the foolishness of preaching to save them that believe" (I Cor. 1:21 KJV). English-speaking churchgoers have long heard Paul's statement in this form. But the New English Bible (like most other recent translations) makes it clear that the sense of Paul's words is, "God chose to save those who have faith by the folly of the Gospel." A gospel has to be proclaimed, of course, and here again Protestants have tended to make the equation: gospel-proclamation equals the act of preaching. Again, Paul's words have been invoked, "How shall they hear without a preacher?" (Rom. 10:14 KJV). But Paul's argument goes on to say, "So then faith cometh by hearing, and hearing by the word of God" (Rom. 10:17 KJV). It is not the preacher of sermons who enables us to hear the gospel. It is God himself through his word. The New English Bible steers us away from making wrong connections in the first place by removing the loaded word *preacher* and translating Paul "And how hear without someone to spread the news?"

Paul follows this question with another, namely, "And how could anyone spread the news without a commission to do so?" (Rom. 10:15). Here the full context for his statements is indicated. It is the Christian church, guided by the Holy Spirit, that proclaims the gospel through her commissioned representatives. Nor does the church proclaim a gospel of her own choosing, but "the faith which God entrusted to his people once for all" (Jude 3). It is because the members of the church "are built upon the foundation laid by the apostles and prophets" — that is, those commissioned to declare God's word to men — that they have heard the good news of peace that Jesus Christ himself came to proclaim (Eph. 2:17).

However obvious this point, it seems to me to be one that is quite crucial to our understanding of the task of the preacher in the church. Christ's church commissions her preachers to represent the Body standing, in obedience to its Head, where God's word is heard. The hearing of this word, through the mediation of the Holy Spirit, produces faith.

The church is not the church without such obedient hearing. And the preacher, through his words, calls the congregation to hear and obey God's word by recalling the gospel that is the faith of the Body of Christ. He is there for the edification of the Body, to instruct its individual members in the faith, to exhort them to continue in the faith, and to rebuke them for their individual and corporate faithlessness. But that is all he can do. The church does not live by preaching. It lives by the gospel, on the foundation laid by the apostles and prophets. The preacher's words are addressed to himself as much as to the congregation in front of him. He, representing the Body, is saying nothing more — and nothing less — than, "This, Lord, is thy word of salvation. This word, Lord, we hear."

A building, then, that is erected for worship and houses a congregation cannot rightly be called a "preaching church." Preaching is one element in the total life of the church. Because the word of God is not only for hearing with the ear and assenting to with the understanding, the preacher in his pulpit cannot represent the wholeness of that word. The word of God was made flesh, and those who receive him are incorporated into him. The sacraments of the church alone can re-present the mystery of that union. The preacher, however, does rightly re-present the faith of the church. The church is nourished on the Scriptures and brought back continually from human wisdom to the mystery of God's salvation. In the offering of its worship the Body of Christ shows forth the Word by which it lives, the Word full of grace and truth (John 1:14). And the preacher speaks for the Body as its representative, witnessing to the truth that sustains the life of the Body in the ceremony of worship.

But, it may be objected, does the preacher not proclaim the gospel as God's very word to men? Does he not seek to bring men to the point of conversion, to preach — as the old phrase has it — "for a verdict"? My reply would be that this is never his primary task. A preacher may be also an evangelist, proclaiming the gospel to those who are not yet members of the Body, or to those who are members only in name. God's word is not bound (I Tim. 2:9), and the Spirit blows where it wills (John 3:8). If individuals happen to be converted to a living faith in the course of worship in a Christian church, this is cause for rejoicing. They may also be converted through having the reality of the faith of the congregation worshiping around them communicated to them. But the purpose of preaching is *in itself* the making visible (or, better, *audible)* of the faith that is in the Body and reminding the members of the Body who are present in worship of the actual content of that faith.

Even edification, which more nearly belongs to the function of preaching in worship than evangelism does, is not essential. It is good, of course, when a sermon sends Mr. Brown away from his pew conscious of his bad temper and determined to do something about it; or when it makes Mrs. Smith realize that she has to apologize to her niece and also become seriously involved in local politics. But primarily the sermon in the context of Christian worship is a symbolic and a ceremonial act. In no way does that imply that the sermon is merely decorative or an unreal going through the motions, which leaves everything as it was before. Because it is a ceremony of Christian worship, it is as real as the ceremony of shaking hands in the context of two people forgiving each other, or as the

symbol of a white flag in the context of a garrison surrendering a fortress.

But if the primary purpose of preaching is not to make
us Christians or even to make us better Christians, though
it may do both, is it then less important than Protestants
often imagine? God forbid! Just as the Body has many
members with differing functions, so the worship offered
by the Body has different elements that combine to make
up the whole structure of worship. Each element has a
part to play if the whole structure is not to be deficient;
and each is honored because it is essential to the whole.

Calvin was surely right when he taught that a full act of
Christian worship ought to include both preaching and the
eucharist. A "preaching service" without the breaking of
bread can only be justified on Augustine's principle,
"Believe and thou hast already eaten." Similarly, eucharist without a sermon can only be justified by the complementary principle, "Eat, and thou hast already believed."
In the former instance, belief needs to include discerning
the Body; while, in the latter instance, eating needs to
include hearing the voice of the one who is the Bread of
Life. The Body of Christ cannot be fully nourished by
worship that re-presents only part of the gospel, even
though every part in a sense embraces every other part.
When the Body is obedient to its Head, it presses on to
"attain to fulness of being, the fulness of God himself"
(Eph. 3:19).

Hearing the Sermon

The church, then, does not live by preaching alone.
Equally, she cannot live without it. In her total life, outside and inside her organizational structures, the church
may use many techniques for evangelism, instruction, and
moral persuasion. But the sermon is integral to her worship, because *sermo* — human discourse — is essential
for receiving grace through faith. The preacher represents
the church for the purpose of re-presenting the gospel in

terms of human discourse — the word of God echoed in the words of men — and he cannot give over his function to, say, a discussion group. The old gibe that the minister in the pulpit is six feet above contradiction states the truth better than it knows. For the word of God, re-presented in the church's worship as preacher and congregation stand before the mystery of the gospel, is not subject to individual approval or disapproval. It is offered for believing reception. The congregation does not necessarily endorse the preacher's stated opinions. It endorses the declaration of obedience to the gospel by the Body that has commissioned the preacher to be its mouthpiece.

The physical setting of the sermon is indeed instructive. Although Protestantism has often neglected visual symbolism in its stress on the centrality of hearing, the traditional central position of the Protestant pulpit is not accidental. (Incidentally, the way the communion table is often made almost invisible by a dominating pulpit points to one of the weaknesses in the tradition.) One man, raised high above his fellows, addresses a gathered congregation, which responds only with an "Amen." "I don't know why people no longer go to church," says one of John Updike's characters, "— whether they have lost the ability to sing or the willingness to listen."[1] What the story in fact suggests is that people have lost the ability to sing in their spirits because they do not have a willingness to listen. One of today's most popular and most misused words is "dialogue." Quite often the mistaken assumption is made that dialogue is good because two people are opening their mouths and expressing an opinion. They are enjoying the opportunity of being heard. But Martin Buber, who first brought the word into popular usage, teaches that dialogue can begin only when the "I" knows that it has been addressed by the Eternal "Thou." Then, and then alone, can there be a true "I-Thou relationship." Dialogue depends on willingness to hear, not on eagerness to be heard.

[1] "Lifeguard," in *Pigeon Feathers and Other Stories* (New York: Knopf, 1962), p. 219.

In preaching the preacher asks us to remember in all he says that we are called upon to be individuals "before God." The gospel is for each of us individually, bringing us into relation with the Eternal so that we can take our place within the Body of Christ in genuine relationship to one another under the Head. The silence of the congregation is not just good manners, or even respect for the calling of the preacher. The congregation is silent because the ceremony of preaching involves, among other things, symbolic listening. In and through the all too human words of the preacher comes the word that makes the listeners truly persons: "Be still and know that I am God" (Ps. 46:10 KJV). To learn to listen is hard, but well worth the price of boredom on the way. Furthermore, boredom is usually as much a result of immaturity on the part of the hearer as of inanity on the part of the speaker. The man who thinks "according to the flesh" finds God the least interesting of subjects to speak *about,* and certainly has no desire to listen *to* his word.

There are endless jokes about sermons putting people to sleep. ("Preaching? Oh, that's just speaking in someone else's sleep!") Yet perhaps we may remember not only Eutychus, who slept while Paul preached (Acts 20:9), but, even more, the disciples, who fell asleep instead of watching with Jesus at Gethsemane. Why, Jesus was not even talking to them — what was there to keep awake for? Listening is really watching in the spirit. And the sermon trains us in such watching; always supposing, of course, that we care to accept the discipline involved. To become disciples in more than name requires of us obedience in many little sacrifices if we are to be ready for the really demanding ones.

If we have lost the art of listening, the reason is intellectual laziness, not education. The smug consignment of the sermon to mothballs because modern man is "too intelligent" docilely to accept what he is told, is without factual basis. Sermons preached by John Donne in Old St. Paul's during the early part of the seventeenth century assumed a breadth of learning that few contemporary college graduates come near to possessing. And sermonic literature down the ages can match for brilliance any other branch of literary creation. No, a much likelier reason that modern man is unwilling to listen is the shortness of his attention-span, conditioned by magazines and television. In church, unfortunately we cannot go channel-hopping. We are reduced to studying the hairs on the back of the neck of the person sitting in front of us, or to reading the notices on the church bulletin. Sermons, like life itself, have to be lived through (or dozed through) to the end.

Listening to sermons, in fact, is an education in reality. It is thus a salutary antidote to the idolatrous attitudes that contemporary culture encourages us to adopt. Reality stretches, indeed, all the way from the vast, overpowering reality of the Eternal God himself to the niggling little realities of having an attack of hiccups in church or finding ourselves irritated by the pitch of a preacher's voice. So it is not surprising that our discussion of the function of preaching has touched both extremes. Because the function of preaching in worship is to be a ceremony that introduces us as listeners to the living God, many of the objections commonly made to it are altogether beside the point. The worth of preaching has really very little to do with whether or not a given sermon succeeds in edifying us. It has even less to do with whether or not it manages to hold our interest or to be "inspirational." The content of the sermon with respect to its acceptability as a human performance cannot be made the basis for deciding to discontinue it or retain it. To use A. G. Hebert's terms, the worth of preaching is not psychological but ontological. So long as men need to listen responsively to the word that addresses them, so long as they are to be brought into relation with the Eternal, the sermon has its place within the worship of the Body of Christ.

Responsible Preaching

The sermon in worship, which is chiefly a ceremony

essential to the structure of worship, is also a means of edifying or building up the Body.

I have argued that its primary function cannot be the moral or even spiritual edification of individual Christians. Rather, it allows individuals to discover that they are part of the Body of Christ, which lives under its Head in obedient responsiveness. For this reason, preaching is properly preaching to a congregation, that is, to a gathering that represents the Body and meets under the direction of commissioned leaders. When Christians meet together for some special purpose like strengthening their spiritual life or discussing some course of Christian action, they may join together in worship. Certainly those assembled can be sure that the Lord is present when they meet in his name (Matt. 18:20), but the structures of such a group's worship will not be the same as those of congregational worship. Indeed, if such a group wishes to affirm its solidarity with the whole Body of believers, it may well proceed to structure its worship so as to include either a sermon or the Lord's supper, or both of these. It is not numbers, after all, but intention that constitutes a Christian congregation. But ordinarily the intention of a Christian group or cell-meeting is not to replace the congregation but to supplement it, and the worship of such a group tends to be directed towards their need for mutual edification.

Though subsidiary, edification is nonetheless a genuine part of congregational worship. Writing to the Corinthian church, Paul warns against the misuse of speaking with tongues in the congregation (I Cor. 14) on the ground that speaking in tongues edifies the individuals involved but not the whole congregation, and that the practice is especially meaningless to any visitor who happens to be there.

The content of a sermon, therefore, is a matter of consequence, even though it cannot be made the basis for determining the "usefulness" of the ceremony of preaching as such. Every sermon, as a human response to the gospel, ought to be a responsible utterance as well as a responsive one. The preacher in his own person represents the freedom of the gospel that he proclaims as one who is responding to God's word. Part of the freedom of the gospel lies in the assurance that the power of God does not lie in any human wisdom. God does not depend on our learning or dialectical skill to make his word effective to salvation. So the preacher need not fear that the inadequacy of his words will make the gospel ineffectual. God uses the foolish things of this world to confound the wise (I Cor. 1:27). A congregation that pours scorn on a preacher's message because, in their opinion, his sermon lacks sophistication and human learning is foolish indeed. On the other hand, the freedom of the gospel is obedient freedom. The preacher cannot assume that the goodwill of his heart will suffice to make the thoughtless words of his mouth into a worthy re-presentation of "God's hidden wisdom" (I Cor. 2:7). If the preacher's words are to edify the congregation, they must be disciplined words, fitting for one commissioned to speak on behalf of the whole Body. As the Reformers were fond of saying, every Christian is a scholar in the school of Christ. The preacher in particular ought not to be a careless scholar in that school. As a steward of the mysteries of God, he has to show himself trustworthy (I Cor. 4:1-2).

In preaching, all the same, the treasure of the gospel is necessarily contained in the earthen vessel of the preacher. Do what he will to speak in obedience to his calling, the preacher still cannot wholly avoid showing in his words his own very fallible wisdom and his own very obnoxious prejudices. His words are received, too, by hearers who possess no more total illumination by the Holy Spirit than he does. It is rather questionable, therefore, to suggest that each individual in a congregation ought to separate out for himself those words in a sermon which are inspired by God and those of merely human origin.

This does not mean, of course, that the reception of any sermon should be one of passive acquiescence on the part of the congregation. If the church is indeed Christ's Body and is indwelt by the Holy Spirit, there must be a "discerning of spirits" within each congregation. A sermon may distress its hearers by bad grammar, bad logic, "irrelevance," and tediousness — and yet re-present Christ. It may astonish us by its brilliance and "contemporaneity" — and yet re-present nothing more than the wisdom of this world. We judge our neighbor always at our peril, as Christ has reminded us (Matt. 7:1). Yet we may be justified in refusing the offering made on our behalf in the pulpit when this offering is offensive to the Spirit that animates the Body of which we are a part. George MacDonald wrote a little poem in the Scots dialect about a minister under whom he had suffered tedium. The poem ends:

> He minded me on Balaam's ass,
> With a differ, ye may ken;
> For the Lord He opened the mouth of the ass
> But this man opened his ain.

MacDonald may possibly have been wrong, but he showed himself a good churchman in not remaining silent over what he considered to be a violation of the sanctity of the Lord's house.

Individual criticism, however, is never enough; and it can be totally destructive of the peace of the congregation. The whole Body must be involved in preserving the health of the Body. It was with this in mind that Bonhoeffer insisted, against the temper of modern opinion, that the church cannot be Christ's church without possessing clear standards for dividing orthodoxy from heresy. Granted that the gospel is not to be identified with ecclesiastical dogmas, it still remains part of the church's service to her Lord to refuse to allow another gospel than the one to which she has been summoned to be preached by her commissioned representatives.

Responsible preaching is always, first and last, faithful preaching. Preacher and sermon alike are symbolic of the faith of the Body of Christ. That is why faithful preaching will always be *scriptural* preaching. By drawing attention to and enlarging on the images of Scripture, the preacher draws the congregation away from the stock responses of spirits enslaved by the false images spread abroad by "the god of this world," and into the freedom of the truth of the God who is real. At the same time, the preacher is a representative of the Body at this period of history. He is our contemporary, and he shares the problems of us, his contemporaries. He has no insight inaccessible to his hearers. His sermon, too, is a contemporary discourse. The words in which it is presented, however traditional many of them may be, have the overtones and resonances of words spoken at this present historical moment. The responsible preacher will not ignore his responsibilities to the present any more than he will turn his back upon the past and discount the wisdom contained in tradition. In order to edify the congregation he will not take refuge in "pulpit platitudes." He will not assure us that Christ is the answer while avoiding the risk and labor involved in analyzing pressing contemporary problems and telling us specifically how Christ comes as the answer to them. Preaching that is responsible can never be vague, can never rest on cloudy generalizations, can never pretend to have the answers to all the vexing questions of the day wrapped up in neat formulas. Edifying the Body means inviting us to enlarge our understanding of ourselves and our world. It invites us to broader sympathies and more comprehensive horizons. It does this, usually less by urging us to carry out policies that the preacher thinks God *must* give his blessing to than by helping us to ignore catchwords and slogans and to use our imaginations to open ourselves to God's truth. Faithful preaching is a means of allowing us to turn away from romantic dreams and the follies of popular ideologies and to turn to the real as it comes from the hand of God.

The Preaching Tradition

Responsible preaching for Christian preachers is preaching that recognizes the preaching tradition. Sermons have

to be made before they can be heard. Even when they
are delivered extempore, they follow a model form.

The most "biblical" of present-day preaching is very
unlike the "sermons" which we find in the New Testament.
Since the time of the early fathers, the model for sermons
in the Western tradition has been, to a large extent, the
classical oration. This form has used the principles of
rhetoric developed in the ancient world to plead a case
effectively. In the nineteenth century, this long-standing
tradition merged with the Romantic cult of the "great
personality" to produce what is often referred to as the
Golden Age of Pulpit Oratory. Then, indeed, the pulpit
and the political platform evolved a similar style, and
frequently influenced each other. This was the time when
Phillips Brooks produced his famous definition of preaching as "truth through personality," and the churches were
filled with hordes of "sermon-tasters" eager to savor the
variety of pulpit personalities about. Sir Henry Irving, the
illustrious Victorian actor, used to go regularly to hear
Joseph Parker preach at the City Temple in London,
though Sir Henry was a declared agnostic. When friends
asked him why he went, he explained it as "the tribute of
one great actor to another."

Today pulpit oratory is not greatly in fashion, though
its appeal is far from dead. We do not grow so many
outstanding personalities in either politics or the church
in the present day as in the days of rugged individualism.
Our so-called TV personalities are pale shadows by comparison, and we tire of them quickly. Yet the Victorian
conception of preaching survived the demise of the Victorian preacher. We still expect preachers to move and
inspire us. There is also an undiminished demand for
"prophetic preachers," by which is usually meant an
orator who gets us worked up over some current issue —
whether it be the threat of a world Communist con-
spiracy or the imperialism of the American war economy
— about which we have already made up our minds anyway. We seldom hail as prophets those preachers who
advise us *not* to throw ourselves wholeheartedly into the

cause we think to be wholly righteous. Jeremiah would have an equally rough time today if he were to contradict those who are quite sure they can discern "where God is in the vanguard and summoning man to freedom and maturity."

There were two men who spoke out against the nineteenth-century pattern of preaching and attacked its basic departure from the gospel message. John Henry Newman strongly criticized the English Evangelical development of preaching from a Catholic standpoint. While appreciating the contribution of the Evangelicals to social righteousness, Newman denounced their emphasis on their subjective consciousness — *their* faith, *their* decision, *their* consciousness of being in a state of grace.

> Poor miserable captives, to whom such doctrine is preached as the Gospel: What! Is *this* the liberty wherewith Christ has made us free, and wherein we stand, the home of our own thoughts, the prison of our own sensations, the province of self, a monotonous confession of what we are by nature, not what Christ is in us, and resting at best not on His love towards us, but in our faith towards Him![2]

Newman saw the beginning of preaching directed towards the arousing of religious feelings instead of a showing-forth of the gospel. At the beginning of this century P. T. Forsyth, a man theologically at the opposite end of the spectrum from Newman, made the same diagnosis of a disease now much further advanced. In Newman's day, preaching was at least doctrinal in intent, if not in performance. By Forsyth's day, traditional doctrines were being tossed aside as outworn garments, and man's own religious aspirations had turned in the direction of high hopes for the future of humanity. Forsyth protested a subjectivism that believed what it thought most important must be what Christianity "really" meant. In *Positive Preaching and the Modern Mind,* Forsyth insists

[2]*Lectures on Justification* (London, 1840), p. 375. Quoted in W. D. White, "John Henry Newman's Critique of Popular Preaching." *The South Atlantic Quarterly,* LXIX, no. 1 (Winter 1970), 114.

that the preacher is free under the gospel and not from it,
and that his first responsibility is to his congregation. He
writes:

> He [the preacher] is not first a prophet of social righteousness
> but an apostle of the Gospel. He is not merely an agent of the
> ethical kingdom. Every Christian is that. But when he adopts the
> ministry as a life work, he adopts what is an office of the Church.
> He becomes something else than a prophet and something more.
> He represents the Spirit which abides like a dove and does not
> swoop like an eagle. . . . His place is not a prerogative of his
> own. It is not a right that belongs to him by his mere subjective
> sense of a Charisma. He is not a wandering seer.[3]

Forsyth realized that the crisis of faith in his age was
the crisis of authority. If the preacher does not stand under
the authority of the gospel, he makes his own subjective
experience his authority and the gospel becomes whatever
the "modern mind" (that was the leading catchword of
Forsyth's day) considers relevant. Meanwhile the church
drifts aimlessly on the eddying current of passing fads and
fancies. Writing sixty years before any secularizing theologian had spoken of the church as "God's *avant-garde*"
and urged us "to see where God is working in the world
today," Forsyth says:

> The Church is not "first of all a working Church." It is a
> communion of saints and lovers, a company of believers, a
> fellowship of spiritual realists. It is there first to feed the soul
> with eternal reality, to establish, strengthen, and settle the soul
> upon the Rock of Ages. You cannot expect ill-fed people to
> devise much wisdom, or do much good. And many in our active
> churches are very hungry as to the soul. They are anaemic in
> in the Spirit. They are fed upon sentiment and not on faith.
> They have hectic energy — and leanness of soul.[4]

It is interesting to see that already in 1907 Forsyth was
sounding the note that the preacher must communicate
reality instead of pandering to the demand for "relevance"

[3]*Positive Preaching and the Modern Mind* (London: Independent Press,
1907), p. 78.
[4]*Ibid.*, p. 119.

by giving people what they want to hear. Just before the passage quoted above, he writes: "A religion that makes men right and real seems to have no chance with one that makes them feel safe and 'good.' " And he adds, "We have to secure our foundations anew."

Securing our foundations anew, of course, is the meaning of standing in a living tradition. Being ignorant of and indifferent to the tradition in which we stand means always perpetuating what is worst in this tradition until it finally dies in our hands. The current complaints about the irrelevance of sermons in worship come largely from an unimaginative assumption that we know beyond doubt what is relevant. And who needs a preacher in a pulpit to tell us what we already know? Only when the preacher tells us things chiming with our prejudices do we feel "good"; and we could get together with a few kindred spirits and raise that good feeling much more easily. Our dissatisfaction with sermons here comes from accepting a corrupt tradition. The preacher is expected to edify his congregation according to the standards of popular demand, instead of according to the standards of reality by faithful response to the God who is real.

The preacher's essential function in the church is to preside over the ceremony of worship in which the congregation is reminded that "faith comes by hearing, and hearing by the word of God." Knowing this, he will not be troubled by complaints that he has become obsolete in a changing world. Trusting the tradition in which he stands, he can help purify this tradition instead of simply debasing it further. He can be always securing the foundations anew, certain that both he himself and the congregation he addresses are certain about why he is there.

So long as the foundations are kept living and real, I do not think that either the matter or the manner of the preacher's preaching will ever cause him ultimate doubts. As a man living in his own times, he will try to understand those times and, in particular, the situation of the congregation he addresses. These are matters of professional competence, and many specialists can advise him

about them. But even if his techniques are poor, his
judgment wanting, and many of his opinions mistaken,
his listeners will find in his preaching a limping grace. It
is not required of preachers that they know everything on
earth. It is required of them that they know something of
heaven, so that they may speak of the one who came
down from heaven (John 3:13) and of the heavenly Jerusalem who is the mother of Christian freedom (Gal. 4:25).
The obedient freedom of preaching is not to be won by
flattering men and confirming them in the comfort of their
own opinions but by being willing to wrestle with angels.

We said earlier that human consciousness is always
aware of living in a three-story universe, even though
contemporary ideologies may teach him to say otherwise
and half believe it.[5] Sooner or later, though, men will
insist upon having some kind of supernatural, some kind
of heaven above the earth and an underworld beneath it.
Their imaginations know better than their theories of the
cosmos what reality is like. The only question is: what
kind of supernatural? What kind of authority, dwelling
either in the heights or in the depths, will men submit to?
If the preacher does not know, his hearers will tire of him
and go elsewhere, confused and dispirited. Christianity,
they will say (as many are now saying), has failed. The
preacher has to know that he is the servant of the church
whose members have here on middle-earth no permanent
home, being seekers after the city that is to come (Heb.
13:14). In the ceremonies of worship men are raised by
the Spirit to see the heaven above, the eternal realm that
gives meaning and substance to our temporal and ambig-
uous world of experience, and know that this eternal world
is sure and abiding. Worship places men in a real relation
to the Eternal. And in the preaching of the eternal and
incarnate Word, human words are given grace to respond
to the enduring truth that is from above.

[5]See above, pp. 167-68.

10

THE MINISTRY OF UNIFYING BONDS

A Fragmented World

One of the most obvious features of current idolatry is that it fragments the human world, both physically and spiritually. The cult of relevance prohibits commerce between the generations and breaks the continuity of traditions. The worship of the Great God Change puts alienation at the center of life, as the world-process rolls on, indifferent to the hopes and fears of the existing individual. The quest for the promised land of liberation puts all human relationships in jeopardy, since each claim that anyone makes on another is thought to be a threat to the other's liberty. The fragmented world is a world where everyone makes nonnegotiable demands, where all bonds — even the bonds of affection, loyalty, and service — are hated fetters, and where human hopes are located entirely in the future, because the present is the sphere ruled by institutions maintaining the oppression of the status quo.

The future itself, in such a world, is as much a threat as a promise. Already casting its shadow over the present in the form of future shock, it promises greater shocks to come. Maybe the ultimate shock will be the world-fragmenting Big Bang. Certainly the most pervasive fear in men's minds today is the fear of a new world war that would mean the mass suicide of humanity. To the fear of

an atomic holocaust is now added the fear of all-out biological warfare, which would end life less violently but as
effectively. To those who respect the truth contained in
images it is plain that these fears for the world do not
exist simply on a physical level. The threat is undoubtedly
real enough on this level; yet the forms of the fears that
we embrace touch us at an imaginative level also, and
thereby gain more power over us. The image of a torn
and splintered earth is a magnified image of our present
experience of a human community disunited and rent by
personal, factional, and international hatreds. The image
of a silent and rotting corpse where the beauty and variety
of nature used to flourish is an extension of our despairing
image of an individual going down to a death from which
there can be no resurrection. The extinction of the world-
process would mean that the Great God Change is not
immutable after all — he too must die. So even the most
widespread of current idolatries offers no comfort to
those who have no other religious faith on which to rely.

I have suggested that, of all the resources available to
man, worship is the most able to bring hope of reuniting
the fragmented pieces of the human world. I have suggested, too, that Christian worship offers a measure of
realism as well as of hope. It does not require us to shut
our eyes to the desolating facts of existence, while it re-
moves their ultimate desolation by placing all threatening
powers under the control of the living God. In the present
chapter I wish to look at the resources of hope and healing found in that Christian ministry which operates in the
sphere traditionally called the pastoral ministry.

That Christian realism concerning the interdependence
of all life is salutary should not be hard to see once we
awaken from deceiving dreams of total liberation. Yet,
more than that, the basic message of the gospel is one of
restoring to wholeness that which has been fragmented.
It is a message of reconciliation. As Paul writes to the
Corinthians, explaining what it means to be "in Christ":

From first to last this has been the work of God. He has recon-

ciled us men to himself through Christ, and he has enlisted us
in this service of reconciliation. What I mean is, that God was
in Christ reconciling the world to himself, no longer holding
men's misdeeds against them, and that he has entrusted us with
the message of reconciliation (II Cor. 5:18-19).

Paul's words sound a note unfamiliar in an age encouraged to think that human problems lie chiefly on the
"secular" level and arise from psychological, social,
economic, and political frustrations. The unfamiliar note
is the suggestion that mankind's primary alienation is
alienation from God, and that all secondary manifestations
of alienation flow from this one.[1] Starting from this basic
theme of an end to alienation from God, Paul goes on
to say:

> We come therefore as Christ's ambassadors. It is as if God were
> appealing to you through us: in Christ's name, we implore you,
> be reconciled to God! Christ was innocent of sin, and yet for
> our sake God made him one with the sinfulness of men, that in
> him we might be made one with the goodness of God himself.
> Sharing in God's work, we urge this appeal upon you: you
> have received the grace of God; do not let it go for nothing.
> . . . The hour of favour has now come; now, I say, has the day
> of deliverance dawned (II Cor. 5:20-21; 6:1-2).

Reconciliation, being made one with the goodness of God
(through the at-one-ment achieved through the cross of
Christ), is at the same time liberty. The obedient liberty
of the Christian is to walk "not as other gentiles walk . . .
being alienated from the life of God . . . because of the
blindness of their heart" (Eph. 4:17, 18 KJV). As the
liberated man wishes to share his freedom with others, so
Paul calls Christians to share in God's work of reconciliation. God's gift of liberation does not set men in com-
petition, but brings them together in a common service.
    This service of reconciliation is the mark and pledge of
the ministry of Christian people to their neighbors.

---

[1]"The conception of alienation was originally a religious one, and perhaps
that is still the context in which it makes most sense." Northrop Frye,
The Modern Century (Toronto: Oxford, 1967), p. 23. The word "alienation," however, owes its present wide currency to the Hegelian philosophical tradition, and specifically to Marxism.

Is a Professional Ministry Obsolete?

Without a doubt, the ministry of reconciliation is the ministry to which all Christians, without exception, are called. There is no question that "the ministry" in this sense is the responsibility of more than just one special class of persons. "Ministry" and "service" here are simply synonyms.

In seeking to take a particular look at the pastoral ministry today, however, I am thinking of Christian service of one special kind, a kind where there *is* a limitation. I am thinking of the ordained clergyman or — to use a secular term which can be misleading (although in my opinion it is perfectly admissible) — the professional minister.

Many concerned people today will argue that the real meaning of Christian service can never appear unless we get rid of the notion that the clergy are a class apart, and that their ministry is somehow different from the ministry of every baptized and believing Christian. Such persons maintain that professionalism in the church is an unmitigated curse that blights its very existence as a true community of equals and makes impossible an honest witness to non-Christian society. The special status of the ordained clergyman, they claim, is a misleading and unjustifiable continuance of an old division between the sacred and the secular, which sprang from the Constantinian establishment of Christianity as a state-recognized religion.

The perpetuation of the division between sacred and secular results, it is argued, in a two-tier stratification of Christians and the ongoing double-standard that there is such a thing as "the Christian calling," according to which the clergy are first-class Christians and the laymen only also-rans. Furthermore, the very fact that some men are set aside for a special vocation means that their witness as Christians is impaired. To be a professional is to be paid, and no one really trusts the sincerity of someone paid to do a job. The more obviously sincere he seems, the more certainly everything that he says or does will be put down to his professionalism. If he goes to the extreme of pouring out his life's blood in complete self-forgetfulness, people will probably say, "Well, he's paid to make it look all very convincing, isn't he?"

Each of these objections has some truth to it. None of them is trivial. Does the combined force of these objections lead to the conclusion that there are good grounds for abolishing — if not an ordained ministry — a professional ministry? I think not.

I believe there are sound reasons for urging a more varied and adaptable ministry to serve the complex needs of the churches in present-day society. The special problems arising out of the nature of this society, with its high mobility and the ever increasing flow of its population towards the great urban centers, obviously demand new patterns of ministerial care. I am also sure that there is room for much increase of lay ministries in areas of service previously considered the preserve of the ordained clergy, as well as for part-time ministries by ordained ministers who earn their living in secular callings. Yet these are all matters of tactics. It is overall strategy that concerns me chiefly. Christ's church on earth is the church militant, fighting from generation to generation a war that never ends. If she is to carry on the war, a realistic assessment of the total resources at her disposal is essential. The traditional ministry is one such resource, and may be more important than is currently imagined.

Once again, our imaginations must be active if false, misleading, or inadequate images are to be avoided. To begin with, the true image of the church's ministry cannot emerge if the ministry is considered simply from the point of view of immediate "usefulness." Making a purely pragmatic estimate of the church's resources means surrendering to the wisdom of this world. If the controlling idea behind an insistence on the equal ministry of all Christians is to transform the church into a democracy where every member is expected to be equally active, worldly wisdom is in control. Just as the church's worship is seen in true perspective only when it is understood as a

symbolic act, so the church's ministry is rightly viewed
only when it is seen as fulfilling a symbolic purpose. The
ordained "professional" minister is a symbolic person.
His function is to represent the presence of the church in
the world.

There is a sense, of course, in which every Christian
does that. Each individual Christian is a member of the
Body of Christ, and, as such, represents the Body. By his
qualities and deficiencies the world judges the character of
the church. Hence the familiar aphorism, "The principal
objection to Christianity is Christians!" But the ordained
minister is an especially commissioned representative. He
represents the Body in a particular way. As we have seen,
when he leads congregational worship he re-presents the
gospel on behalf of the whole congregation. He has there
a special symbolic function to perform, one which makes
the act of worship a corporate act of the whole Body.
Similarly, in the pastoral office he re-presents symbolically
the church's presence in the world in a manner different
from the day-to-day witness of the lay Christian. The difference does not lie in his being in himself a special kind
of person and decidedly not in his being a specially
advanced spiritual personality or a more "Christian" Christian than the layman. It lies solely in the symbolic significance of his commissioning. Other Christians may be
commissioned by the church for special kinds of Christian
service; he is commissioned to represent the church as a
whole.

There is considerable resistance at present to the idea
of a representative person. So many features of modern
living oppose the idea that our imaginations will hardly
take it in. To be sure, traditional Western democracy
rests on the notion of representative government. But that
tradition is now suspect. The ideal of so-called participatory democracy is lauded — that, in principle at least, all
important decisions should be made not by the elected
representatives of the people but by the people themselves,
recording their immediate judgment on issues as they arise.
In most spheres of life, individuals resent strongly the

assumption that they are bound by any policies made on their behalf by others unless they themselves have personally signified their agreement. Indeed, representation is seen less as safeguarding liberties for the individual than as threatening his independence. Representation, after all, by its very nature involves delegated authority; and the notion of authority is widely held today to contradict individual liberty. The cry goes up, "Who is to tell me what I ought to do (think, believe, agree to)?" The liberty to be solely responsible for one's own decisions is thought to be the most fundamental of all liberties.

Nevertheless, there is good reason to think that such a view is confused, and that it arises from a failure in imagination to comprehend the realities of the human situation. Because of this failure we embark on our quest for total liberation, ignoring the interrelatedness and interdependency of persons in actual existence. Then convinced of the impossibility of reconciling authority with responsible freedom, we of necessity encourage atomistic individualism — or its complementary opposite, mass conformity — and thus destroy the possibility of healing relationships that could truly reconcile individuals and create real community. I believe that recognition of the minister in his symbolic role as the representative person of the Christian community could be an important step in reversing this fatal trend. Once our imaginations become flexible enough to embrace such an image, we may discover that it has implications for every sphere of human relations.

The Authority That Serves

That the Christian gospel denies atomistic individualism is plain from the fact that at its heart lies the atonement in which "one man died for all" (II Cor. 5:14). While the gospel of the crucified Christ has always been an offense, the substitutionary atonement has been especially offensive to the modern moralist who thinks in individualistic terms. In his Preface to *Androcles and the Lion,* George Bernard Shaw clearly imagines that his readers will agree with him as a matter of course when he writes:

> Consequently, even if it were mentally possible for all of us to believe in the Atonement, we should have to cry off it, as we evidently have a right to do. Every man to whom salvation is offered has an inalienable natural right to say "No, thank you: I prefer to retain my full moral responsibility: it is not good for me to be able to load a scapegoat with my sins: I should be less careful how I committed them if I knew they would cost me nothing."[2]

Shaw wrote that in 1915, when he could count on the stock response of imaginations conditioned by nineteenth-century individualism and rationalism. So he argued on the basis of a *natural right* to refuse atonement because it would sap individual moral initiative. But Shaw, at least, had no pretensions to being Christian. He did not view Jesus as a Savior but as a moral teacher whose teachings had been perverted by the religious fanaticism of Paul. Few people today would admit allegiance to the nineteenth-century dogma of rugged individualism. At the same time, the atomistic moral vision that this dogma popularized has come to dominate the consciousness of men to such an extent that even those who are within the Christian community frequently show an attitude toward the atonement as naive and simplistic as that of Shaw. Bultmann, for example, dismisses the concept of substitutionary atonement as mythological, without advancing a scrap of evidence that it is. Bultmann evidently assumes that anything lying beyond the range of the "contemporary" imagination possesses the primitive character belonging to mythic thinking. It certainly simplifies thinking to say, "I don't see anything in it, so it's a myth!" Yet such a variant of the ostrich stance is hardly the best way of facing life realistically or of discovering the complexities of actual existence.

In actual existence the individual always stands in relation to others and finds his individuality by admitting and

[2] *Androcles and the Lion. Overruled. Pygmalion* (London: Constable, 1931), pp. 92-93.

extending the bonds of personal relationships. Christian
faith teaches us that our primary relation is always to the
living God. In Kierkegaard's phrase, the individual becomes an individual *before God*. The Christian finds his
relationship with God in Christ through belonging to the
Body of which Christ is the Head. Calvin insisted that no
one can have God for his father who does not have the
church for his mother.[3] Life in the church is a life in relationships. It is a life where freedom and obligation, independence and obedience, responsibility and acceptance of
authority go hand in hand, related, not set over against
one another as enemies.

An atomistic moralism considers the free gift of God's
forgiving grace an infringement of our right to stand on
our own feet and exercise full moral responsibility. Quite
otherwise, the Christian community is inspired to action by
the reminder, "What do you possess that was not given
you?" (I Cor. 4:7). The spirit of the world assures us that
we will be less careful about our sins if we know they cost
us nothing. The spirit of Christian faith calls us to costly
service on the basis of the message: "You do not belong
to yourselves; you were bought at a price" (I Cor. 6:19-20).
The gospel is a call for us to assume our responsibilities
precisely because it is an announcement of what has been
done for us to allow us to become responsible beings. Man
did not create himself; and, having unmade himself through
sin, he cannot save himself. Therefore, the seemingly strong

[3]*Institutes*, IV, i, 1. It is a great loss to the Protestant imagination that in
reaction to Roman usages, it has largely given up speaking of Mother
Church. Calvin did not hesitate to apply to the church all the images of
motherhood, writing: "Let us learn, from her single title of Mother, how
useful, nay, how necessary the knowledge of her is, since there is no other
means of entering into life unless she conceive us in the womb and give us
birth, unless she nourish us at her breasts, and, in short, keep us under her
charge and government, until, divested of mortal flesh, we become like the
angels (Matt. 22:20)" (*ibid.*, IV, i, 4).

To refer to the church as "she" instead of "it" may seem rather artificial
in these prosaic times of ours. Yet it may be all the more needful when
we are so much oppressed by a sense of the impersonality of the world
around us. And let us not think that "a little thing like that" does not
matter either way. Verbal images have mighty potency, and the difference
between "it" and "she" is vast in terms of imaginative effectiveness.

and liberating hope that man can and will save himself is in reality an irresponsible counsel of despair. The truly liberating hope is in the gospel of our redemption in Jesus Christ:

> For it is by his grace you are saved, through trusting him; it is not your own doing. It is God's gift, not a reward for work done. There is nothing for anyone to boast of. For we are God's handiwork, created in Christ Jesus to devote ourselves to the good deeds for which God has designed us (Eph. 2:8-10).

Thus freedom within the Body of Christ comes from the knowledge that its members share the completeness of their obligation to receive all from the Head. The members of the Body receive their individual independence of action through their willingness to "compel every human thought to surrender in obedience to Christ" (II Cor. 10:5). Similarly, within the Body acceptance of authority is not felt as an alien imposition, but as a summons to enter into the liberty of the sons of God. Christ, the one who spoke with authority (Matt. 7:29) and called for obedience (John 14:15), was also the one who came to serve (Matt. 20:28; Luke 22:27; Phil. 2:5-11) and to give men the gift of life in all its fulness (John 10:10). Obedience to the Lord is not burdensome but liberating (I John 5:3).

Any attempt to come to grips with the issue of the church's commissioned ministry has to begin with the terms of the church's commission under the gospel. The ministry of the church necessarily reflects the life by which the church lives. When we speak, in the traditional way, of "holy orders," the reference may be in part to ecclesiastical structures, indicating the rules laid down for the ministry by church authorities. But, beyond that, there is a reference to the total ordering of the Body of Christ under its Head. When this larger pattern is forgotten, the distinction between clergy and laity may indeed become a man-made ordinance, one that divides the Body of Christ and obscures the universal ministry of the Body. But it does not follow that the distinction is meaningless and ought to be discarded; for it is witness to the unity through relationships which constitutes the true ordering of the Christian community. The commissioned ministry gives a visible image of that authority whose recognition makes a Christian congregation an authentic part of the church of Jesus Christ. The authority of the ministry reflects the authority of Christ himself, who sought not to dominate or compel but to serve (Matt. 20:25-28).

In speaking of "the order in which the Lord has been pleased that his Church should be governed," Calvin points out how good a training in humility and in charity God gives us "when he accustoms us to obey his word though preached by men like ourselves, or, it may be, our inferiors in worth." He stresses in particular, however, how the unity of the church is expressed in the ministry. He writes:

> For did every man suffice for himself, and stand in no need of another's aid (such is the pride of human intellect), each would despise all others, and be in his turn despised. The Lord, therefore, has astricted his Church to what he foresaw would be the strongest bond of unity when he deposited the doctrine of eternal life and salvation with men, that by their hands he might communicate it to others . . . Whoever, therefore, studies to abolish this order and kind of government of which we speak, or disparages it as of minor importance, plots the devastation, or rather the ruin and destruction, of the Church. For neither are the light and heat of the sun, nor meat and drink, so necessary to sustain and cherish the present life, as is the apostolical and pastoral office to preserve a Church in the earth (*Institutes*, IV, iii, 1, 2).

To the objection that Calvin's age was different from ours, and that what seemed important to him may not seem so to us, I would answer that this makes it all the more necessary for us to listen attentively to his words. When Calvin wrote, the medieval understanding of the corporate nature of all human society was still present not only in men's minds but in their imaginations also. Without much imaginative effort they could appreciate Paul's image of the church as the Body of Christ made up of various "members" or organs. Today, when our thinking about society oscillates between atomistic individualism and mass collectivism, we find it difficult to capture the same vision. In a fragmented world that has come to consider "authority" as a superfluous relic of the past — since any and every type of authority is seen as a denial of individual freedom and responsibility — we need to rediscover the healing function of an authority that serves.

The Pastor: A Representative Person

In arguing that a truly human freedom cannot be attained without obedient acceptance of bonds that unify the human family, I have suggested that this principle — so essential in the life of the church — holds good for all areas of life. The need for the recognition of authority stands under this same principle.

Wherever the very existence of a community is at stake, the need for obedience to authority is beyond question. This can be seen, for example, on a ship at sea, where the captain is in absolute control. Also, now that we have been made aware by ecologists of our precarious situation as we journey together on Spaceship Earth, we are ready to listen to those who can speak with authority on the subject of our corporate survival. These examples serve to show that a genuine authority is never authoritarian (in the pejorative sense) but is an authority that serves.

Thus the opposition often made between trusting in authorities (seen as a bad thing) and forming our own opinions (seen as a good thing) is usually a false one. In fact, trust in authorities is a measure of realism necessary to our corporate survival. We need to trust in authorities because we are social beings. Individually we cannot know everything necessary in order to keep alive and maintain our well-being. Thus, we have to depend continually on the special knowledge of others by acknowledging their authority where they have a wisdom that we lack. Those who speak contemptuously about "blind faith in authority" will, nevertheless, if the occasion arises, agree quite docilely to submit themselves to an operation simply because a doctor says that it is necessary. So-called blind trust is not the same thing as credulity, and very often may be the reasonable and responsible course. Certainly, we have a duty to find out whether any supposed authority is worthy of our trust. We *are* blindly credulous if we submit ourselves to a bogus authority. Here, incidentally, is where we are most dependent on the existence of continuous traditions. We are able to trust a sea captain or a doctor chiefly because of the ancient and living traditions maintained by their professional organizations. By way of contrast, the ecologist is a johnny-come-lately; and so in the matter of environmental pollution we are faced by conflicting "authorities" and loud-mouthed charlatans, who often gain a wider hearing than less colorful and more cautious experts who do not claim complete authority for their utterances.

Sea captains and medical doctors are representative persons because they possess specific skills. They also have a symbolic status, as can be seen from the prominent part that both professions have always played in fiction and on the stage and screen. Today, in popular entertainment, the doctor is in a class by himself. Hospital series form as large a part of television viewing as they do, not simply because of the drama of the operating room, but because the doctor is a convenient symbol of the wise and caring person — the loving father or protective elder brother — who is largely absent from our impersonal, technologically organized world. The hospital is itself an image of that world: huge, sterile, as much a maze of endless corridors as Kafka's nightmare castle, full of unknown workers going about their tasks with impersonal efficiency, a repository for countless forbidding machines, and a place where people find themselves brought against their will. Into this place of fear and pain comes the doctor, the Good Samaritan who will comfort and mend in body and in soul the unfortunates who have fallen among the dreaded robbers of our age: illness, old age, and loneliness.

The present elevation of the symbolic role of the doctor above his functional role comes, I am convinced, because of the withdrawal of the minister from his proper role, a role that ought to be primarily symbolic. I am also convinced that this withdrawal has been more a voluntary one than the result of any change forced on the minister by the spirit of the age. All too often, the minister seeks to make up for his lost symbolic image by qualifying as a professionally trained "counselor." I would not wish to demean the place for such specialized training in the ranks of the professional ministry. But the question of priorities is vital. And, whereas some ministers ought also to be experts in counseling, all ought to be professional *pastors* — and most to attempt no more (and no less) than that. Yet, as I see it, this is the full-time professional task that is in the process of becoming the exception rather than the rule. To represent the church of Jesus Christ and to re-present the ministry of reconciliation by his presence in a particular locality is no longer considered the minister's principal task. He must prove his "usefulness" to the community, in ways that are other than symbolic of his office, and in directions that can meet some pragmatic test.

The word "parson" simply means person. The parson in his parish was originally *ecclesiae persona,* "the person of the church" in his locality. He represented the ministry of the church by what he was, rather than by anything that he did. Of course, he did a great deal; and, since he was often the best educated person around, he was generally active in all kinds of "secular" matters. But first and last his work was to be the representative person of the church both inside and outside the church building. Where he went, the church went; wherever he was present the comfort, discipline, and unifying presence of the Holy Spirit indwelling the church was re-presented. Certainly, the faithful minister was expected to be also a truly representative Christian individual. Because he led the congregation in worship, he himself had to be a worshiping person. Because he preached the gospel of reconciliation, he himself had to be a reconciling person, one exhibiting in his personal life the fruits of the Spirit. Nevertheless, it was always understood that the personal deficiencies of the minister did not invalidate his representative status.

If it is thought that this tradition of the minister as the representative person of the church is no longer relevant to the contemporary situation, this may well be because the uniqueness of our times is overestimated and the constant needs of the human spirit are underestimated. Moreover, the chief resistance to the recovery of the tradition is likely to be found among ministers, who for some time now have been actively engaged in trying to get rid of the image of the minister as someone different from the layman. Under the mistaken notion that the representative person is the same as the preeminent individual, they have been insisting that the minister must on no account be "put on a pedestal." He is to be just another Christian in the congregation — at best, "a resource person" or an "enabler" helping his fellow-Christians engage in constructive service to the community. When lay people agree to such an image of the ministry, they usually do so, rather ironically, under the impression that the minister knows best. They still preserve an instinctive (though unformulated) conviction that the minister *is* "different."

Any other image of the ministry except that of representation claims both too much and too little. It claims too much, since ultimately there is no other resource person for the church except Christ, and no enabler except the Holy Spirit. The minister can re-present Christ and the Holy Spirit; he cannot replace them. The church as an agency for "social change" is no better — and for the most part much less efficient — than other cultural groups in society, and it reflects the same culturally conditioned limitations they do. But the image of the ministry that fails to recognize its function of representation claims far too little, for it denies to the minister the right to speak with authority to the world about the one subject on which he has the right to speak authoritatively, namely, the reconciling power of God's word.

These days we hear much about the need for "Christian presence." Perhaps it would be better if we heard

more about the need for "Christian representation" or
"churchly presence." The best commendation of Christian
faith that can be made is undoubtedly a life of Christian
service that reflects the spirit of dedication to the works of
love and evidences the living presence of the mind of
Christ in one of his servants. Yet for an individual to set
out consciously to be a missionary of the gospel by being
a "Christ" to·his brothers and so draw them to faith: this
is of necessity a program founded on pride, if not presumption. The Christian minister in his representative and
symbolic role does not presume to be such an individual.
He simply enters on that sphere of service to which he
believes he has been called by the Holy Spirit. He does not
think that he is worthy for his task. He is called to it in
spite of his unworthiness, not because of any pretense to
spiritual preeminence. He embarks on his calling when his
sense of vocation is ratified by the church. He continues in
it subject always to the discipline of his brothers in the
faith. He may and should possess missionary zeal. Yet his
calling is not in the first place to be a Christian individual
commending the church by his life. His calling is to represent the church and to symbolize her presence in the world.

When the minister regards himself as being the representative person of the church in a locality, he is claiming
nothing for himself individually. The sole claim that he
makes is to be recognized as a person specially commissioned by the church. That is, he acknowledges his symbolic
status. And here he can and ought to speak with authority.
His authority, all the same, belongs to him wholly by
virtue of his representative function. As an individual he
is simply a member of the Body of Christ like every other
Christian.

The Authority of Representation

Each representative person whose authority is publicly
recognized and established by tradition is tempted to misuse the authority delegated to him. A ship's captain may

turn into a Captain Bligh. A head of state may turn into an Adolf Hitler. In the history of the church the evil of authority transformed from authority-to-serve into authority-to-tyrannize calls to mind a very real abuse that goes by the name of *clericalism*. This memory has made the idea of the minister as the representative person of the church so distasteful that it has been largely set aside as unacceptable and even unthinkable.

Yet, once again, the principle holds good that the use of anything should never be determined by its abuse. Clericalism is not at all a present danger for us. The loss of the meaning of the ministry as a unique calling is a real and actual danger.

We are seeing in the example of the Roman Catholic Church how catastrophic is the loss of a tradition of clerical authority. It is catastrophic even when that tradition stands in urgent need of revision and reconstruction. On the psychological level, indeed, it is particularly catastrophic in such circumstances. The "crisis in authority" affecting Roman Catholicism from the papacy down to the parish priesthood and the seminaries reflects a loss of trust in the hierarchical system of ministerial orders developed through the centuries in that church tradition. The rejection of Roman "triumphalism" from within the system might be thought to be pure gain; and, in the end, it may prove to have been a purgation well worth all the turmoil that it has occasioned. Yet in the meantime there is evidence that not simply one theory of orders but the whole conception of ministry has been undermined to such a degree that constructive reform has been endangered. Confusion over the meaning of churchly "vocations" is evidenced by the drastic decline in candidates for the priesthood and for the monastic orders.

Protestantism has suffered no comparable shock. The decline in ministerial candidates has been a phenomenon that the Protestant churches have been living with, off and on, through most of this century. The twin phenomena of the grouping together of rural churches and the closing of many "white elephant" buildings in the inner city have masked the shrinkage of number, while the influx of ministerial candidates during the later forties and fifties still provides a cushion against feeling any acute dearth of pastors. And there has been nothing like the spate of clerical defections (frequently because of a decision to marry) experienced in the Roman Catholic Church, even though the major Protestant denominations continue annually to lose a considerable number of ministers who no longer have confidence in their calling or simply see a secular life as more worthwhile. The total picture of the Protestant ministry is hardly a reassuring one.

The authority of the minister as a representative person is derived from the authority of the reconciling word. That authority is confessed by the church as the authority by which she lives. Under the direction of the Head, the Body of Christ is committed to the ministry of reconciliation. In his representative capacity the minister symbolizes that ministry and thus shares in the delegated authority belonging to it. As long as this aspect of the ministry remains unrecognized, the image of the ministry will remain confused and impoverished. Calvin insisted that disparaging the ministry by not seeing in it the means God has willed to use in the salvation of mankind is inviting the ruin of the church.[4] The church is corrupted when her ministers become authoritarian and behave as though they, either individually or corporately, possess authority to rule over the laity like masters over servants. Yet the church loses her identity and her very reason for existence when her ministers lose the sense of having authority because, as representatives of Christ's Body, they re-present the reconciling word.

Calvin saw the ministry to be "the strongest bond of unity" in the life of the church. In a fragmented world we desperately need to recover a vision of the unity of human existence. In a world that has turned so largely to an idolatrous vision of total liberation we need to relearn the need for bonds that do not enslave us at all but can

---

[4]See above, p. 213.

unite us in the freedom of true personal relationships. Better than anything else could do, a recognition of the ministry as embodying the authority of the reconciling word gives us assurance of that unity-in-freedom. In his capacity as the representative person of the church the minister mediates the ministry of reconciling bonds.

The notion of the minister as a mediator may strike the Protestant imagination as an image too "Catholic" to be acceptable. Was not the Protestant Reformation itself a protest against the quasi-pagan concept that the priest is an intermediary between the individual and the redeeming God? To this objection I think it suffices to note that the Reformation's repudiation of clericalism was not a repudiation of the authority of the Christian minister. Protestant belief in the priesthood of all believers did not exclude differences of function within the Body of Christ. The Reformers never intended that clerical authoritarianism be substituted for with an atomistic individualism that finds no necessary role for the church and her ministry. That particular development in some later Protestant thinking was a complete departure from the Reformation vision and a corruption of the Protestant tradition.

In the Protestant tradition no name given to the minister is more honored than that of "pastor." Yet no one except Christ is truly worthy to bear that name, for he alone is the Shepherd of the flock and the one whom the sheep follow (John 10:2-5). In being called the pastor the minister does not usurp the place belonging to Christ. Similarly, the mediation of the minister does not compete with the unique authority of Christ as the one Mediator between God and man. Paul indicated the mediatorial work of his own ministry when he called himself an ambassador, writing: "We come therefore as Christ's ambassadors. It is as if God were appealing to you through us" (II Cor. 5:20). The minister does not mediate salvation. He mediates the ministry to which all those who have been saved by Christ are called. He does so in his pastoral work by re-presenting the unity of the Body of Christ, the unity

that the people of God enjoy by accepting Christ's yoke of
obedient freedom.

By definition, the authority of the ministry can be nothing
other than authority to serve. Yet it is, nonetheless, authority. Through the pastoral ministry of her ministers the
church calls the flock to follow the way of unity that is
found in Christ. Through these ambassadors God himself
appeals to men. Simply by being faithful Christians all of
us can find opportunity for serving our neighbors. But
service with authority belongs peculiarly to the representative person of the church, the commissioned minister.
This is because the minister, when he performs his work
of pastoral care, is not merely a Christian individual. He
also fills his symbolic role.

Both in his preaching and in carrying out his pastoral
duties, the minister trafficks in actualities as well as in symbols. The activities of a pastor, indeed, are intimately
bound up with the concrete actualities of human life. He
has to encounter people in specific situations involving
particular stresses and emotional reactions. He cannot
help being personally concerned in each of these situations.
He has to weep with those who mourn and rejoice with
those who are glad. Thus his individual qualities, his
strengths and his weaknesses, become evident in his pastoral work. In all relationships with persons, personality
matters a great deal. That is why some men are more
"successful" in the pastoral ministry than others are.
There are born pastors as there are born preachers. Their
personalities incline them to this aspect of ministry, and
they feel themselves at home in it.

At the same time, whenever the pastoral office is tied
too closely to the individual personality of the pastor there
is a real danger of misunderstanding his office and so of
bringing it under the power of the spirits of this world.
Just as "truth through personality" is not an adequate
definition of preaching, so "edification through personality"
is not an adequate definition of pastoral care.

It might seem to be. I have argued that the edification
of individuals, though an important part of preaching, is

not its primary purpose. Preaching is directed first of all to the congregation, the people of God assembled for worship.[5] The pastoral ministry, however, is the care of persons. It seeks to build up individuals and families into a mature faith (Eph. 4:11-16). To this end, the pastor has to enter into personal relationship with the members of his flock and with any person with whom he comes into contact in the course of exercising his ministry. Thus edification through personality might seem to be the very essence of his work. Nevertheless, all true edification can only be the work of the Holy Spirit. "Not by might, nor by power, but by my spirit, saith the LORD of hosts" (Zech. 4:6 KJV). The power of personality should be included within this warning. The pastor who depends on a warm and sympathetic personality to do the work of edification may be successful in the eyes of the world. He may win the praise of men and perhaps their admiring affection also. Yet it may also happen that (in Milton's words), "The hungry sheep look up and are not fed."

The Pastor: the Man and the Office

Because he is a representative person, the pastor symbolizes the church in its care for its members and in its love for all men for whom Christ died. That is why the minister exercises his pastoral role because of what he is (representatively) rather than because of anything that he does. His presence by itself is the sign of the presence of the concerned and serving church, the church of the Good Shepherd who knows his own sheep by name (John 10:3) and sees that not one of them is lost (John 17:12). When this symbolism is recognized, the personal deficiencies of the pastor as an individual matter very little by comparison.

It would be absurd to suggest that these shortcomings do not matter at all. Though edification through personality does not define adequately the pastoral office, yet pastoral

[5]See above, pp. 190-91, 194.

care, even more than preaching, is a highly personal task. In the pastoral ministry it is impossible — and undesirable — to divorce completely the symbol from the individual man. For example, a bereaved person may be in great need of an answer to the question, "If a man die, shall he live again?" He will not be edified to receive an answer on the general grounds of "what the Church teaches." Still less will he be edified if he has the impression that the pastor himself has no personal conviction of the truth of the words which he relays, and that he is individually untouched either by the presence of human sorrow or by the divine power of the Resurrection.

All this is simply to say that symbol and actuality meet in the person of the pastor. When the actuality contradicts the symbol, the symbol cannot be effective; or, at any rate, it is subject to the severest strain. Especially in these days when the whole idea of a representative person is foreign to men's imaginations, there are very few who are able to draw strength from the authority of the symbolic presence of the church in an individual whose personal integrity they find questionable.

Nevertheless, this state of affairs does not make meaningless the symbolic role of the pastor. It makes the need for a recovery of the recognition of that role the more urgent. There is, after all, a very fine line between passing judgment on an individual's personal integrity and objecting to his personal idiosyncrasies or finding his temperament uncongenial. It is a scandal for the church when her ministers are conspicuously failing in living personal faith, dedication to their sphere of service, and genuine human compassion. Yet, when it comes to entire worthiness to represent the mind of Christ in the world, who is worthy?

In the Protestant tradition there has always been a strong reluctance to isolate the dignity of the "office" of ministry from the character of the minister. This has been a strength in preventing the symbolic role of the minister from becoming a form without a living content expressed in a dedicated human existence. In practice, however, this strength has frequently become a weakness, one which has resulted in esteeming man's works higher than God's grace. Laymen have been encouraged to glory in the talents of the minister, in his capacity for leadership, his effective oratory, and his ability "to get along with people." Small wonder that, in reaction, Protestants have begun to question the function of the "professional" ministry and to ask whether the Body of Christ would not be better served by abolishing the distinction between clerical and lay Christians.

In these circumstances it may seem perverse to suggest that the cure for the malaise that has infected the ministry should not be looked for in the direction of abolishing the ministry but in the direction of making it more professional. Yet I would suggest just that.

I am not talking about increased training for ministers or about their being expected to gain additional professional "skills." A professional man is one who professes or acknowledges a specific calling or vocation demanding his full-time service. A professional calling is contrasted with following a trade or business for one's own economic advantage. In this sense, the minister is a professional man. I am convinced that the image of the ministry needed today is an image that magnifies the *calling* of the minister, an image that stresses his office rather than his personal qualities. Instead of imagining that anything dividing him from the Christian layman makes him a less effective witness to Christian faith, the minister ought to believe in his special calling. Without any apology, he should profess himself to be a cleric.

My conviction arises from the manifest need today for a recovery of the sense of the church as the Body of Christ. Society in our day is fragmented by the outlook of atomized individualism — an outlook that encourages a flight into its complementary opposite of mass collectivism. In such a society the individual claims the right to total freedom but remains unfree and haunted by the specter of alienation. The church of Jesus Christ offers a better image of society, the image of a society founded on mutual care and trust through the free obedience of the Body to its Head.

The minister (or professional cleric) alone can symbolize adequately the unity of the church as a society bound together by reconciling bonds. Lacking such an effective symbol, the church can present to the world no more than the image of a collection of Christian individuals. The combined goodwill and good works of such a collectivity can never be sufficient to show the church to be the Body that lives by God's free grace and "thus knit together grows according to God's design" (Col. 2:19).

The pastor, in particular, is the visible representation of the church as a reconciling Body in the midst of the fragmented world. For he moves in this world, carrying his ministry to those who long for fellowship and find nothing but loneliness. He is a living, walking symbol of the church that is in the world but not of the world. He is the concrete image of the ministry of the Body that is obedient to its Head. Christ's own ministry was to seek and save what is lost (Luke 19:10) with an authority that serves. To this end he rebuked the proud, comforted the sorrowful, and taught that man does not live by bread alone. And this ministry, which is the ministry committed to the whole Body, is symbolically re-presented in the person of the minister.

It may be objected that this is not at all the image suggested by the minister in these days. The presently prevailing image is rather one of the ineffective do-gooder, of the innocent idealist shielded from the tough realities of life; or else, it is one of the purveyor of irrelevant religiosity and out-of-date moralism. These images, however, arise from viewing the minister as a conspicuous individual Christian who is expected conspicuously to embody the Christian virtues. As such, he can hardly do anything that will not tarnish the image of the "genuine" Christian. If he tries to follow literally the command to "give when you are asked to give" (Matt. 5:42), he is sneered at as an easy touch for the panhandler; if he tries to discriminate, he is condemned as a hypocrite who does not practice what he preaches. If he mixes freely with the unchurched, trying to be "all things to all men" (I Cor.

9:22 KJV), he is accused of seeking a cheap popularity; if he is concerned to give a specifically Christian witness, he is labeled pompously pious and a religious bigot.

Christ himself, contrasting his style of ministry with that of John the Baptist, remarked that it is impossible for any individual to escape the derogatory personal image (Luke 7:31-35). Any image, in fact, can be changed only when it is superseded by another image. Suppose that, by some miracle, every minister in the world were suddenly to be transformed into a perfect Christian. The old images of ministerial inadequacy and hypocrisy would almost certainly continue exactly as before. It really matters very little what the present popular image of the minister happens to be. What matters is that the minister himself maintains a true image of his ministry. So long as he sees himself as the representative person of the church rather than as the would-be exemplar of Christian character, he is encouraging an alternative image to take root in men's imaginations. Hopefully, this better image may spread abroad in society at large. Yet, even if such a desirable result does not follow, a cause of confusion will have been removed within the church. Christ was less concerned about the images the contemporary world had of him than he was about how his own disciples imaged him (Mark 8:27-29).

Jesus Christ is unique because his office and his person are one and indivisible. He is Christ and Lord because he is the eternal Son of God who became incarnate in the person of Jesus. No one else except the individual who was named Jesus of Nazareth carries the name that is above every name (Acts 4:14). Christ's ministers do not have that unique status. While their individual lives should be in conformity with the honor of their office, their authority lies in their office and not in their persons. The true image of the ministry can emerge only when this truth is consciously and emphatically affirmed.

The Reformation of Images

Few would dissent from the Reformation principle

ecclesia semper reformanda — the church stands in need of continual reform. The heirs of the Roman Catholic tradition as well as the heirs of the Protestant tradition acknowledge its validity. Reformation is always needed in the church to counter the idolatrous tendencies that infiltrate the Body of Christ and turn it away from obedience to its Head.

But the crucial question is always "reformation in what direction?" If my analysis throughout the present study carries any cogency, the direction in which reformation is needed should be evident. Reformation in the church means, among other things, turning away from the stock images of the contemporary imagination to learn anew the realistic images of biblical revelation. Paul wrote to the Christians at Rome:

> Adapt yourselves no longer to the pattern of this present world, but let your minds be remade and your whole nature thus transformed. Then you will be able to discern the will of God, and to know what is good, acceptable, and perfect (Rom. 12:2).

The transformation of our minds, I have argued, depends more than a little on the transformation of the images of our imagination. Adequate, biblically based symbols can prevent us from adapting ourselves to the pattern of this present world by pointing us to a better pattern, which is God's will for us.

Reformation has to begin with the church. If the church will not listen obediently to the word, the world cannot be expected to have the opportunity of hearing it. This is why I have suggested that the reformation of images can best begin with a reexamination of the images connected with the church's ministry. Here, if anywhere, is an opportunity for resisting conformity to the pattern of the present age through listening to the spirits that dominate it. Here is a call to turn from the idols that exercise power over contemporary imaginations and to recover the power of God's word mediated through the images of Scripture. For the living God has willed that these images should be the means of our laying hold of saving truth and being led to Jesus Christ, who is the image of the invisible God (Col. 1:15).

INDEX OF NAMES

INDEX OF SUBJECTS